ROB CALLOWAY

All American Prizefighter

Amazing Things Press

Book design by Julie L. Casey

ISBN 978-0692586105
Printed in the United States of America.

For more information, visit
www.amazingthingspress.com

This book is dedicated to my beautiful wife, Robin Rae, My Champ, Chase Samuel, and my beautiful daughter, Riley Rae.

Thank you
I love you

ROUND
1

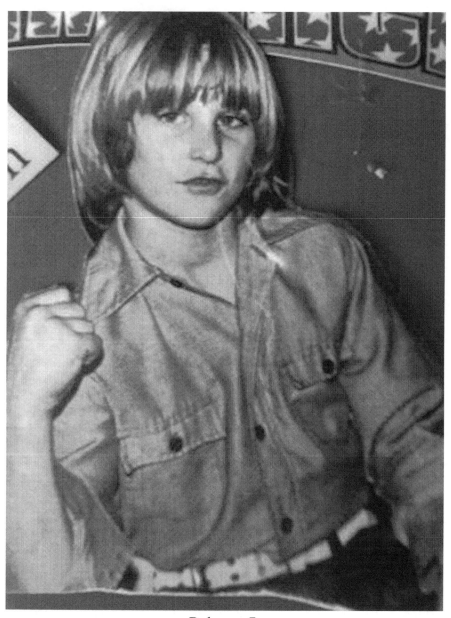

Rob, age 7

Mike and Rob Calloway

7:00 Pm Thursday, October 25th, 2012

I'm sitting in a hotel room in Arkansas—not waiting for an upcoming fight but arrived earlier this week to begin my first travel assignment as a Licensed Physical Therapist Assistant for Med-Travelers, the health care company that hired me last week. I'm here in Mountain Home, Arkansas for the next 12 weeks, driving the five hours home as often as possible for the weekend to see my beautiful wife of 21 years, Robin Rae Calloway, our son Chase Samuel Calloway who will be 17 years old in less than two weeks, and Riley Rae 'Butter' Calloway who is 15 years old. I hope I enjoy this new job traveling around the country doing Physical Therapy and I really think I will. Some may think it beats the hell out of traveling around the world to fight some of the best fighters on earth but to be honest, I really miss it and I think I still have a few more fights left in me...I'm only 43 years old; maybe I could...OK, I admit it's over.

I report to Pine Lane Therapy and Living Center, a Retirement Community, to assist residents in rehabilitation including ambulation with an assistive device if needed and exercise instruction to help gain strength and improve balance and overall safety to improve their daily lives. I love this job and it's about as opposite from the sport I loved and dedicated much of my life to for the last 25 years as it could be.

Wow, what a crazy ride I've been on. I feel I finally have come to accept my boxing career is over. I lived a dream, a dream that I actually had many times as a young kid in Kentucky and sitting here looking back, I have to admit I've loved every bit of it and I thank GOD I'm still healthy with body and mind. I—Charles Robert Michael Calloway—Robbie Calloway—Rob Calloway became the All American Prizefighter. I hope everyone enjoys the story of my life the way I remember it...

5

I was born in Hartford, Kentucky July 18th, 1969. As I've tried to look back to my earliest memories, I'm stuck at age 5 in 1974 when Muhammad Ali won the World Heavyweight Championship for the second time in Zaire, Africa versus George Foreman. I guess I remember the fight mainly because we lived in Louisville, Kentucky, the home of Ali, and at the time I remember the excitement from family members every time 'The Greatest' would step into the ring over the next several years. My Louisville residency did not last long as my family moved many times throughout my childhood. I attended four different third grades in two different states—Kentucky and Oregon—and I could not remember living in the same house for two Christmas's from the time I was born until I moved to Missouri at the age of 17. I was forced to grow up early and now I truly believe GOD had a plan for me and gave me a stubborn mind with the tenacity to understand that I will get out of life what I put into it, so I never complain about what I was not given and I made my mind up at a very young age that I was going to be successful—the honest way—no matter what.

My family moved back to Hartford, Kentucky where I started grade school at Wayland Alexander in Miss Taylor's class. We lived in a trailer park in Owensboro, Kentucky and then soon moved back to Ohio County to attend a couple different grade schools. Soon I was introduced to the police through my father, who I now understand wanted to be successful just as I did, but found it too hard to overcome the obstacles in his path. My dad, Mike Calloway, was the oldest of five boys and his father also had several brothers and a sister.

I soon understood that one big reason no man in my family had been successful was that none had an education or respect for it. I remember one time after getting one of my third grade report cards, I began crying in the car because of the D's and F's and my dad said, "Shut up, why in the hell are you crying?"

My mom replied, "Well he wanted to do better."

"I have never seen a man cry over getting bad grades," Dad said.

My mother explained, "He is not a man. He is a nine-year-old boy." Then she said to me, "Different schools are at different levels. You were just a little behind this school and have not had much study time on a few of the subjects, so don't feel bad. We are moving to Oregon and maybe you will be ahead of that third grade when you get started." Well, I can't remember being ahead of schedule, but it made me feel better anyway and I was always proud that in all the different schools we attended from then on, I never failed a class and graduated on time in 1987 at Ohio County High School at the age of 17. I didn't turn 18 until that summer on July 18th.

I've always respected and loved my mom for many reasons. She was married at 15 years old and had me the following year. With the many tough paths she has had to walk in her life, she was always a provider and protector of her kids and I thank her and will always love her for that. Many times in my career, I would think about her toughness and her sacrifice for us when I was motivating myself for a fight, and she is, perhaps, one of the reasons I never allowed myself to give less than all I could. 100% win or lose, that was the way it was for me. I thought of many more life experiences along the way during my career that would motivate me prior to fights but many times, I would look back to my childhood for motivation. It was in the third grade, as young as I was, that I learned how important education was and I wanted to do my best. I'm sure many boxing fans still do not know I have a college degree in Physical Therapy and was the first Calloway to graduate high school from our family.

I remember hearing the stories of all the trouble my dad and his brothers and even my grandpa and his brothers would cause around our towns. My grandpa would brag about knocking out the Sheriff's two front teeth one night when he came to pick him up once again for drinking too much and causing trouble.

My dad and his brother Curtis seemed to be close and find trouble together often. We spent several months visiting dad in jail and even one time at the hospital after the police came to our door and said they had taken Mike to the hospital from the jail cell. I remember the police coming to the door on another occasion to tell the family that my uncle Curtis had been released to the hospital from jail, if only for a short

7

time. I guess it was worth it.

I remember my dad being in trouble with the Law from time I was a toddler until I left for Missouri at 17 years old while he was in a maximum-security prison in Southern Kentucky.

I realized also at a very early age this was not the life for me and should not be glorified, as it was nothing more than an easy way out. I have stated many times that it is easy to do things you shouldn't do, like steal, bully people who can't defend themselves, etc., but it was hard to do the right thing, like get up every day and go to work on time or school when you didn't really have to go, or simply to not misbehave and follow the rules as we are expected to. Although that seems pretty simple, it's not, and the people who are able to do that every day are the so-called tough ones that I respect.

I never really understood why I have always liked fighting so much and never had a fear of it. I must have gained confidence at a very young age, maybe just through life experiences when you can either be embarrassed and shy or you can stand up and fight back if treated in a way you disagree with. I always stood up ready to argue or fight for what I believed. I gained a reputation at a young age, and there were times I may have been too aggressive to someone. I look back now after retirement and hope I never hurt anyone's feelings too much as a young kid. I think it must have been a combination of being a Calloway and coping with the negative attention brought on by my family and having to live with people thinking we were different or white trash. I heard that comment several times as a youngster and took offense to it, even though some in my family would laugh it off.

I was also very close to my mother's four younger brothers as she had seven brothers and three sisters, one who died as a baby. My mother was the youngest of the girls. Her father, my grandpa Everett Lindsey, passed away at a young age from black lung from working in coal mines for years long before they had protective gear. I always heard of his hard-working attitude and his pride of having a large family. I was told he was very small in stature, only 5'6" maybe, therefore Little Man was his nickname. I was only around 2 years old when he passed away so I do not remember him.

My grandmother remarried later in life. I remember going to her home in Hartford and later to her and her new husband's home in Rosine, Kentucky. I was never a fan of her new husband. Even at a young age, I developed the attitude that I shouldn't say I am close to or a friend to someone I am not. Charles, My grandmother's husband, passed away years later and my grandmother lived many years after that. She was able to visit her children and I felt she always had a lot of love for her children, grandchildren, and soon great grandchildren.

My dad found trouble often and soon it became normal for us to visit him in jail and then prison. This went on for a few years and from time to time he would make parole. He had an aunt in the state of Oregon who told him there was ranch work there and he was welcome to bring his family out and start over, which he did. But it didn't take long for the small town life and hard ranch work to make him decide the move was a mistake. We packed up and returned to Kentucky during that school year. That would lead to another small Kentucky town and then another and another. I was enrolled in four third grade classes that year. I began to see it's easy to steal from people or cheat but success is what happens when hard work and motivation meet ambition. I ask myself what's ambition? I think it means willingness to work for what you aspire to be, fight for what you want, never give up, never quit, strive to be the best.

Mike and Curtis soon got back together and began to plan a way to get rich quick and along the way would end up arrested again with similar charges as Curtis was sent to Eddyville in southern Kentucky and Mike to LaGrange in Louisville and shortly to Blackburn for good behavior. I remember his stay at Blackburn, a minimum-security prison. He would often escape at night. One time I saw him and he assured me all was good. He told me to go back to sleep and he'd see me the next morning as we visited him at Blackburn.

Later, Mike escaped and took the family back to Oregon, and I began my fourth grade year once again in Mitchell, Oregon the very small town south of Portland. My dad was on the run from the police and soon my Great Aunt Flossie turned him in. Our school year was over and he was transported back to Kentucky to face charges. This left my mother to drive back to Kentucky with me, a 10-year-old getting ready to start the fifth grade, my sister, two years younger than me, and now a younger brother, Jonathon. My mom was nine months pregnant with her fourth child, another boy, Karl Patrick Calloway on the way. She also agreed to let a 15-year-old girl who had her permit come along to help drive if Mom needed help driving. I remember we stayed in Kentucky with Mike's parents, my grandma and grandpa, who lived in a small shack at the time. They moved often as well, and my grandmother was the only one that worked as far back as I could remember on my dad's side of the family. We spent several weeks there in the four-room little shack sleeping on the floor at nights.

I looked forward to the nights when my uncle Jeff, my dad's youngest brother, would take me with him out on the town. I enjoyed being a dumb teenager who was actually only 10, or 11, or 12. It did not take long for me to realize I didn't enjoy sleeping in a shack and I wanted to be something one day. I don't remember anyone ever speaking of having goals of getting out of the miserable circumstance they were forced to live in, as if it was almost destiny that no one with last name of Calloway was ever allowed to be successful.

I remember the men in my family cursing and using the word *nigger* like it was a given they were better because of the color of their skin even though they were considered white trash by the white people in our city. I could not understand this even at a young age. My family lived in the projects while my dad was in prison and I became best friends with mostly black guys and I had several girlfriends, both black and white. I would fight anyone at the drop of a dime if they showed disrespect to my sister or me. Their skin color didn't matter, I think, because I stayed with my friends and neighbors, and it was easy to see we are the same race...the human race.

I would speak of Muhammad Ali and I would say the next Ali was going to be Greg Page. He won the National Golden Gloves and he spars with Muhammad now, so just wait and see. My friends would act like I was crazy and wanted to talk basketball or football. They didn't care too much about boxing and never heard of Greg Page. My Uncle Jeff, my dad's youngest brother, only cared about getting girls to party, smoking some weed, and drinking, so I would follow along. It embarrasses me to admit some of the things I experimented with not only that summer but the next and next until we eventually found ourselves living in Ohio County, Kentucky again.

School, of course, was never mentioned and even as a very young kid I wondered what my uncle was going to do with his life. I saw my dad and all of his brothers being in legal trouble as long as I could remember and all had families and kids at such a young age. I just thought that was the normal thing to do. I began to look forward to nighttime, as I knew soon I would load up in the car with Jeff and his friends. They all had girls who like to party and I was allowed to say I was 13 and that I had been smoking and drinking for years. Everyone else had been, but I was actually only 10, 11, or 12, depending on the summer, as we would return to visit during the summers often. Some weekends, my uncle would drive to the local bootleggers—Ohio County is a Dry County—or we would have to get alcohol in Owensboro if we did not go to the bootleggers. At times I would get to drive us all home as I would only have one beer because I really didn't like the taste of it. I only drank it because I thought the 15- or 16-year-old girls thought it was cool, especially the way I cruised and smoked a cigarette at the same time. In the summers of the late 70's and early 80's, we would go to the Strip Pits and swim, of course watching out for snakes swimming in the water. If we saw any, we would choose to go to the next pit a few miles down and swim if there were not any in that pit at the time.

My dad was being transferred to a minimum security prison between Lexington and Georgetown, Kentucky, and my mom decided to move us all to Georgetown, as it would be close to Blackburn Correctional complex and we would be able to visit my dad more often.

ROUND
2

We lived in Georgetown from my fifth grade year
grade year in several different houses or apartment com
during that time I felt like I became who I am today in many ways. v. -
lived in the projects called Boston Park and when asked if I played
basketball, I said. "Hell Yeah, of course!" I had never played any basketball as we had never lived in area long enough with my dad on the
run from police or in prison, and I'm sure I had never even shot a basketball. I tried out for the team that year in the fifth grade at Garth
elementary and of course I did not make the team. I remember how
terrible I felt not making the basketball team; I remember never wanting to feel like I was not good enough again in basketball or whatever I
wanted in life, so living in the projects and playing basketball with my
friends, I practiced almost daily until I became pretty good. We actually moved several times but usually in same area just across the town
to a better apartment building, Scroggins Park, so I had the ballpark
right there. I had no rules with my dad in Prison and my mom working
and then taking care of two baby brothers and my younger sister, who
did the baby-sitting when my mother was not home. I decided I was
going to not only make the basketball team next year, but I was going
to be good. I had developed a desire to be the best I could be at whatever I decided to do. I would even walk across town to Georgetown
College as their dorms had basketball courts outside, so when I was
unable to sneak into the gym to shoot some ball, I would settle for the
outdoor courts by the dorms.

I remember playing on the school league just like I did playing in
the park outdoors with the neighborhood kids: I was usually one of the
youngest and only white boy, so I learned to be aggressive and play
my best all the time. I won the MVP my sixth grade year which was
my first year of basketball. Our neighbor at the time was impressed
after my mother had told him of me winning the MVP and noticed me
walking to Georgetown College to shoot basketball almost daily. He
would speak to me on occasion and one day said, "Robbie, Kyle Macy
is having a basketball camp at Georgetown College in few weeks and

you would like to go, I'll ask people at my church to help get you there." I don't remember his name, but I remember the generosity he offered and I feel I made the most of it as it was the sport that would bring me to St. Joseph, Missouri and allow me to meet my beautiful wife.

"Do Your Best at Every Thing Every Time. Live Right. Ask yourself, 'Is what I'm doing right or wrong?' You already know the answer!!!! Do the Right Thing! If you get good at making excuses, it's difficult to excel at anything else!!!!"

I have often said all these year, "If Being a Champ was easy, it wouldn't mean as much to be called a Champ."

In my sixth grade year at Garth Elementary, I was voted the MVP of our team and Bret Berrup, a Kentucky basketball player who was our guest speaker, awarded me the trophy. My basketball coach was Dale Stowe and one of the greatest things I have found about Face-book is I have had the chance to tell him of my success in the sport of basketball in high school, which brought me to Missouri and allowed me to follow my dream of boxing.

Coach said my boxing career does not surprise him a bit as he remembers me being a very tough kid. He remembered saying at the awards banquet how tough a kid I was for winning the team MVP trophy in my first year of organized basketball after not making the team the year before. He also said at the banquet, "If I told Robbie to run his head through that wall right there or said I didn't know if he could, then Robbie would do it."

I like to work my mind and use my memory, so I want to share a joke Bret Berrup told that night of the awards banquet when I was given MVP trophy in my first year of organized sports.

He said his friend, who was another Kentucky basketball player we were all aware of, was working at a grocery store during the summer, and a big ugly guy came in and wanted a HALF HEAD OF

LETTUCE. His friend told the customer, "Let me check with the manager," so as he walked to the back of store, not realizing the big guy was following him. He got to the manager and said, "Excuse me, but there is this REAL BIG HUGE FAT MAN, I MEAN THE UGLIEST GUY I HAVE EVER SEEN IN MY LIFE, WHO IS WANTING TO BUY A 'HALF' HEAD OF LETTUCE. He noticed the manager was a little nervous and his eyes were looking behind the young ball player so the ball player turned around. Then he turned back to the manager and said, "OH YEAH, THIS GUY WANTS TO BUY THE OTHER HALF!!!!!!!!"

I've always remembered that story... I also always respect smart people; it's always been important to me that I made the most of my mind as well as my body after I got into college.

I had already had several fights as a youngster in Oregon or trying to impress my uncles in Kentucky. On one occasion at a family reunion, we decided to have a family baseball game in the city park and eventually it was my turn to bat. Two guys just a little older than me were behind the fence at home plate and began chanting "easy out easy out." I got so pissed off, I threw the bat behind me to the fence and charged right around it.

Many of my family members did not know what was going on, but my mom's youngest brother Ferlin, who was seven years older than me told me, "If they keep giving you shit, take care of it." Ferlin said he would make sure only one got involved. I moved around the home plate fence and the family gathered near home plate on their side of fence trying to see what had just happened. I came up to the kid who had decided he would be the one of the two to step up. I already had my Dukes up ready to throw punches and I did—several in a row to his face. Then the kid got away and picked up a really big rock. Ferlin said he better not hit me with that rock so as the kid looked at him, I took the rock and threw it away. Again I put my dukes up and threw some straight punches. The two took off, leaving me a champ at fighting for the first time in front of my family, which I felt they respected more than any other sport.

WC, one of my uncles, I remember told the story to some friends of his. He said, "Rob looked liked ALI coming around that fence with his fists up by his face." He then said the next Muhammad Ali would be Greg Page, then maybe Rob next. Greg would never become Ali of course, but would go on to win a heavyweight title. Hearing my uncle speak of Greg, it did not take me long to want to learn all I could about Greg Page and I too became a fan of his.

My father soon made parole and began working as one of the projects' maintenance men, which I considered respectable. My mother began taking some college courses at Georgetown as she had got her GED and enjoyed going for a short time. But it did not last long as Mike didn't like her being on campus very long, to say the least.

I continued playing basketball in seventh and eighth grades and started playing football as well. I loved the competition of sports and football was my favorite. I was aggressive in both basketball and football, even though I was really not very talented, in my opinion, as other players were better than me. I just think my hustling and aggressive play was something the coaches always liked so I rarely came out. I only remember my dad watching me play one basketball game and that was the first basketball game I ever played in sixth grade. He never got to see me play football. I continued to be a starter in basketball and up until I graduated eighth grade. By that time, my dad had decided to take the family back to Ohio County where we started.

I made several great friends in Georgetown, including many I have touched base with through Facebook, which I found to be so great for reconnecting with people from my past. I found out through Facebook that one of my best friends, Richard Honaker, from grade school had passed away in vehicle accident.

I remember Richard walking into fifth grade class with his friend Shing Webb, who would later become one of my best friends as well. They both looked like tough street kids and I guess I was too, which brought us all together. I found out about Richard's death through Michelle, a grade school girlfriend from the same projects. Michelle also said she remains friends with Shing. Michelle told me I had always protected her, so it didn't surprise her that I became a professional fighter because I was always fighting. I would begin to dream of playing college basketball or even football through eighth grade. The thought of boxing soon began to fade away as it was not a popular sport to kids around my age at the time or at least in the area I was in.

I had another good friend, Robert Green, who was friends with Richard and me. Robert and I were respected for not only playing football and basketball, but also for being tough kids who were not afraid to fight anyone. One day we got mad at each other for something silly in our homeroom class and it became an argument that escalated into meeting at the Garth Grade School playground about a mile from our Scott County, Georgetown Middle School. By the time school had ended, word got around and hundreds of school kids followed us to the fight. The first punch took a while to be thrown, but eventually we both landed our fair share of punches and neither went to the ground. The next day at school, I had a black eye that looked bad and Robert did as well but with his black skin I told him it didn't look as bad. We became even better friends the last few months before I returned to my birthplace of Ohio County.

I recently became Facebook friends with Robert, who is doing well and loved hearing about my boxing career. I told Robert I wanted to let him know that I remembered he was a southpaw and I had trouble with left-handers my entire career. He had a good laugh.

That summer, before leaving, I remember playing baseball in front of Richard's apartment complex. A kid walked by and said he heard I said he stole my bike and I better quit talking shit. Well this kid was 16 years old and had already quit school and I was not even 13 yet, but several girls were playing with us and with my best friend Richard and several others. I said "Yeah, I did because I saw you with it at the pool." I had seen him, but why couldn't I keep my mouth shut? This would be another time in my life I realized I was meant to be who I became because although he was older, bigger, had a reputation, etc., I stood up to him. He had on mirror shades and when he came up to me and pushed as hard as he could, which almost knocked me down, I put my fist up and started swinging lefts and rights as hard and fast as I could. I broke his glasses and cut his face and although he left knuckle prints on my cheeks from his punches, I was considered a champ by fighting him. He had to have stitches from the glass cuts to his cheek. I was a champ again.

I enjoyed my 4 years in Georgetown Kentucky and I'm so happy with Facebook to be able to touch base with my old friends again and to let them know I remember them just as they have remembered me. My wife got upset as I was talking to them as if they were still fifth-eighth graders. Robin said, "Robbie," as she is the only one that calls me that besides these Lil Girls from Georgetown, Kentucky. I'm not sure she liked that too much, but Robin said these Lil Girls are now women in their 40's and some divorced etc. I realized she was right again but I really have always thought of them—Jackie, Anessa, Anne, Michelle—as pre-teens still.

I've loved having an opportunity to touch base with Shing as well, who was one of my best friends as a young kid. We were both sorry we lost another close friend, Richard, in a car accident.

I also lost another friend, my best friend, Samuel Chelsey Johnson, in a car accident. I was blessed that my wife, Robin, agreed to name our son Chase Samuel as Robin had met Sam the summer after my freshman year of college and she saw how good a guy he was after only meeting him one night. Sam was always a tough young man and I thought of him all through my career. That would never allow me to give less than 100% and quitting was never an option. I always thought to myself that Sam doesn't get to live life anymore; I get to fight for a Living. I Always did my best in every fight. I always wanted to win and ALWAYS believed I would win prior to the first bell ringing in all 92 professional fights I've had around the world. We were just kids, but Sam was a tough young man and we felt the same about many things in life.

All American Prize Fighter Rob Calloway 40 Amateur and 92 Professional Fights...76-14-2...60 Wins by Knock Out! Love Ya Sam!

People may find it hard to believe I actually thought of the people or circumstances I did while training or motivating myself prior to fights. I fought in St. Joseph a lot but I also fought out of town a lot and would even train away from home to prepare. Our minds are so awesome as I would always want to win simply for my wife and the opportunity to offer our children the best life possible. I also had a chip on my shoulder that it was not someone else's fight but my own. I did not feel good enough about myself and would take offense if someone said they thought someone was better than me.

I really liked to box—fight—as I always felt we competitors were 100% equal in the ring. We had both signed a contract weeks before and we both agreed to fight and understood that a win would allow us to make more money for our families in the next bout. Some may think it's odd or 'lil krazy' but I Looked at each boxing match as a fight and I remember one guy I fought from our hometown late in my career saying he messed up by fighting mad. I never understood that, as I was mad every time I fought and considered every match a fight. Oh well, it sure is fun to look back on my career now, knowing I did my best every single time I got in the ring.

NO EXCUSES: GET GOOD AT MAKING EXCUSES IT'S DIFFICULT TO EXCEL AT ANYTHING ELSE.

ROUND
3

Me, Samuel Chelsey Johnson, Reggie Kennedy, David

The summer ended and we moved back to where we started in Hartford, Kentucky in 1983, spring break of my eighth grade year. I finished eighth grade at Ohio County Middle School then I started the summer with girls, partying, drinking, and smoking with many who had graduated high school that year on my mind. But soon I began to hang with my friends more and with some of my family members less. As Reggie spoke of wanting to play college football, I began to have the same dream. He, Sam, and I would start on defense as sophomores. In a fairly large high school with a graduating class of over 200, that was rarely accomplished.

In the ninth Grade at Ohio County High School, I joined the freshman football team and still remember going undefeated. I made friends with guys who are still some of my best friends to this day. Reggie, who I was best friends with in first, second, and third grades became my best friend again as soon as I moved back.

I remember our undefeated freshman season as well as our coach being a dumbass who I guess thought paddling us for saying the word 'man' made him feel better about himself or maybe feel lil bigger or taller as he was short guy. One time I said 'OH MAN' before practice after hearing one of my favorite teams got beat in college football so he said, "Ok Calloway, you're next." I said, "Really?" He said, "You said 'man,' didn't you?" I said, "Accidentally, as Kentucky got beat and was winning." He said, "So what? Come inside." So I went inside our locker room as well as the rest of the team and he spanked my ass, just like he did several others on team only he left a red bruise on the cheek of my ass. I pray one day he reads my book and if you do, Coach Salyer, please look me up one day. I'm not a 14-year-old Freshman in high school anymore, however, I'm 6'3, 225lbs with 40 amateur fights and 92 professional fights, fighting five World Heavyweight Champions, winning the WBF World Heavyweight Championship by beating Big Bob Mirovic on the Gold Coast of Australia in Fox Sports 2005 Fight of the Year. I have 60 of my 76 wins by knockout. Don't try and take credit for my meanness as life made me this way Not You, Bitch.

Thank GOD no teacher, coach, relative or anyone else ever whipped my son's ass for saying the word 'man' or anything else as I guarantee I would knock every one of the bastard's teeth out. I'm not joking; I'm very serious.

I love my mom as she stood up for me at the time.

I don't have to say anything about any man in my family.

I said my mom stood up for me.

You are Appreciated...

Soon Reggie, Sam, and I were named All State on defense our senior year. I was the only senior football player that played high school basketball that year as well. I remember one of our big games in basketball, the seniors had picked whoever they wanted to wear their football jersey to our Homecoming game and Sam said, "Calloway, give me your Jersey as us real men who play Football instead of basketball are all going to cheer you on tomorrow night." Most of the other players chose a girlfriend, but Sam wore mine.... Although I was high point scorer and led the team in rebounding, I felt it was because I was just aggressive and very tough. That allowed me to get several awards, including MVP, my senior year to go along with being named All State in Kentucky in both football and basketball. I earned a few scholarships to some small colleges down south and could have gone to play college football, which was actually my favorite sport to play, but I still had a crazy dream one day I was going to be a Boxer. I remember going to basketball camp my senior year. I was voted to be on the All Star Team from camp and was even given a starting position at shooting guard. The other All Stars were superstars like Rex Chapman, who graduated the year before but agreed to play with us as his dad was the head basketball coach of the college where we were having our team camp. The other starters were great basketball players like Travis Ford and Felton Spencer who would all go on to have great college and professional careers. I had a good high school experience in sports and wished I were more serious with my grades all through school at that time as I graduated with barely a 2.0 GPA. On my first ACT test, I scored a 12, and Coach Winkler said, "You must have a score of 15 to play college basketball so you best quit hanging out all night and get home get some sleep and study so you can improve." He scheduled me for the next available test, which was in Owensboro. I drove over and was able to make an 18 that time.

I never took the ACT test again as that was the minimum score to get into PTA school as well and I only needed a 15 to play college sports so I was done. I always think about our children making in the high 20's and Robin expecting them both to make 30's. I said," I'm satisfied, Robin, both of them scored great." She said, "They are both capable of scoring higher." I said, "I ever tell you what I scored?" She said, "Yes you have and please don't repeat to our kids." I said, "Has Anybody Told You They Love You Today Robin? I Do!"

I was home one night and happened to have the TV on. I was looking forward to the big fight I had spoken about, but no one really seemed interested but me at the time. Mike Tyson vs. Trevor Berbick for the World Heavyweight Championship. Mike won impressively, becoming the youngest heavyweight champion in history and begin a Hall of Fame career. That night I told my mom I was going to go to

Tarkio College, a small college north of Kansas City so I could have a chance to box as I really thought I could be good. I knew how to fight and I'd boxed a lot as my parents had given me my first pair of boxing gloves. I kept them in my car in case anyone wanted to try me out.

My mother had divorced my dad after he got arrested again and married Ralph Goodwine who had become a friend to my mom while working at the Dairy Queen beside our high school my senior year. Mom did not believe my promise of pursuing boxing, but she did not question me as I had already achieved so much in sports as well as being first Calloway to graduate high school.

I loved sports and had a drive to be the best I could and my mom was just happy I agreed to go to college and get an education. I rarely stayed home when I was a teen as my girlfriend had an apartment and had graduated two years before me. I was always welcomed to come and stay the night until I was caught running around with other girls in her car while she was working at Walmart. I'm embarrassed to say the silly things a teenager will do if not given supervision by an adult they respect. I know my mom loved me and my sister and brothers and did her best at the time but it was very hard to control a young man with huge ambitions who seemed to be on his way and who had no fear of failing or needing to return home.

I became best friends with Reggie Kennedy, the same best friend I had in first, second, and third grade before we moved away. Reggie had an older brother, Robert, and a younger brother, Shane, who were great athletes as well as Reggie. Reg got out of the county on a football scholarship to play linebacker at Murray State University in SW Kentucky. He had had a tough upbringing as many of us did at that time, however, I don't think his dad, nicknamed BadEye, was ever in trouble with the law but had a reputation for being a tough SOB and I always respected him. I remember watching Marvelous Marvin Hagler fight at Reggie's house one day as I spent the night quite often. BadEye commented that Hagler was the best fighter he ever saw.

I followed Hagler from that day on and he became one of my favorites. I still love watching the Great Fights of Marvelous Marvin who got cheated out of that fight with Sugar Ray. I knew that would get it started as what a great fight. Many may not remember, but Hagler fought right-handed the first few rounds for some crazy reason, as he was a great southpaw.

Oh well, I love Sugar Ray Leonard and after meeting him and the way he showed so much love and respect to my son on his birthday when we took Donny to the Contender Finale. I'm reminded how much I love the sport of boxing every time I think about that trip and how much fun it was for our son Chase to meet all the great Contenders. They were all just good hard-working young men trying to make a name for themselves the most honest way—fighting.

Reggie got the chance to come to one of my fights in New Orleans, but it got cancelled the day before the fight. Reg had already arrived with some friends from his work so we had a great time in New Orleans and talking about the old times. I still keep in touch with Reg and am so happy he is successful with two beautiful little girls and a wife, Michelle, whom I never met but always liked. When I won the World Championship in Australia, I sent several VCR tapes to some close friends, including Reg. He said Michelle cried after watching it as I spoke of love for Robin, Chase, and Riley after winning a very emotional 2005' Fox Sports Fight of the Year on the Gold Coast of Australia.

I'm looking forward to seeing my best friend Reg as I'm working in Texas on Louisiana Line now, only a couple hours from him in Houston. Very soon Robin and I will have a double date with them in Houston!

I had another great friend, Tim Berry, who I went to Grade School at Wayland with and he was also good friends with Reggie. We all three got together again once I moved back to Ohio County from Georgetown. Tim was a very good football player as well and although he moved away to Tennessee after our freshman year, I was very honored we kept in touch and he was able to come to my first retirement fight in St. Joseph, Missouri and was able to hang out in the locker room and walk to the ring with us. I was glad he got to see his old high school friend live the dream of becoming a boxing champ as well as getting to marry his best friend, Robin Rae and have two beautiful children. I'm so happy Tim, who himself excelled with athletics and used his mind to became a doctor. I'm very proud of him as I know how far he came from that trailer in Hartford, Kentucky and hope he was proud of his old friend. I've loved keeping in touch with old friends and just as Reggie told me, "Rob, Old Friends are the best,"

when he and I first touched base again.

I also met and became best friends with another linebacker, Samuel Chelsey Johnson, Sam and I became close and enjoyed hanging out together and by the time we were seniors in high school, it would be very seldom you would see one without the other. Sam was a very tough kid and thought he could beat up anyone.

He would often say, "Rob, if we ever get into it I'm taking you straight to the ground because I'm not going to stand up and box your ass." I had never even boxed in a sanction match at that time but always had boxing gloves in trunk of my car like my uncles who also had no amateur boxing training but loved the sport—or maybe just the idea of being a real boxer who could fight.

I am so happy my wife Robin got to meet my best friend Samuel Chelsey after my freshman year of college, although Sam passed away just a week later in a car accident on his way to work one morning in Oklahoma. Robin could see we were special friends and years later agreed to name our son Chase Samuel Calloway. We even had Chelsey Rae Calloway picked out for Riley until a few minutes after she was born and Robin said her name is Riley Rae and I agreed. I've never regretted giving Chase Samuel his name and I think Robin has always loved the name very much as well.

ROUND
4

I moved to Tarkio, Missouri at the age of 17 when my high school basketball coach Steve Winkler brought me to Tarkio College to visit the school, coach and team, and play some pickup ball in the practice gym in front of all of the coaches. I impressed them as they picked up I knew how to handle myself on the court with confidence and aggression with the basketball. I could also dunk pretty well back in the day and I was never afraid to show off anytime I got the chance. I have always respected Coach Steve Winkler for his dedication to trying his best to make us the best basketball players we could be, as well as teach us how to become better young men through respect and hard work. Coach Steve would take me to several other colleges around our area that were interested in me playing basketball for them and I even was recruited to play defensive back in football at a few small colleges since I was named All State in both football and basketball. But soon I made up my mind it would be Tarkio to play basketball as I still had the dream of becoming a boxer.

Coach Steve and I remained friends and kept in touch even though he moved and became a high school coach for another school. I even visited his new school to play some pickup games with him and his team after my freshman season. I had told Coach I was planning on signing up for the Kansas City Golden Gloves after the season was over when we came to visit the college together. That was one of the reasons I wanted to come to Tarkio because it's near Kansas City and I thought Kansas City has the Golden Gloves. I always wanted to try to become a boxer as I really thought I could be good. Coach Steve agreed and said that sounds great and although wished me the best, I'm not sure he ever felt I would take my boxing career to this level. Even I never realized I would be able to take my boxing career to the level of success I've had.

I'm always setting goals and then I feel like it's my responsibility to make the goals I've set happen. It's on me. I never blame anyone for anything I was not given or something I was unable to attain as I truly feel GOD gave me my mind, athletic ability, healthy body, fighting heart, and the rest is up to me to make to most of it.

I've always acted big, tall, like wanting to take the basketball to the hole as there was not a 3-point line in high school when I was there or I wanted to run the football up the middle if possible and I wanted to fight and be Heavyweight Champion of the World. After my freshman year of college, I was 6'1 175 pounds and I was 18, almost 19 years old. I grew another 2 inches and would fight most of my 20 years as a professional fighter in the Heavyweight division.

I always wanted to be Heavyweight Champion. Louisville Kentucky must put big egos in young men that live there as kids— Muhammad Ali, Greg Page, Rob Calloway. I had to mention my name with two other heavyweight champions and Muhammad Ali of course, being 'The Greatest of All Time.' Sorry, but it is my autobiography

Coach Steve was like a big brother that I had respect for as he took me to sign up with the college I chose to play basketball for and he made it a big deal at our local high school when I had my signing day. We stayed in touch for years and as my boxing career began to excel, he was one of the first to congratulate me after watching me on television. I enjoyed playing college basketball and remember listening to the Tyson Fights on the radio on one of the college bus trips to a basketball tournament. I was a Tyson fan like many at that time and would tell the coaches and teammates about watching when he won the World Championship my senior year of high school and deciding I was going to Tarkio to play basketball so I could attempt Kansas City Golden Gloves one day. Coach Steve and his wife Sue who I began to love as she was always a fan of mine playing basketball and I could tell her boyfriend and soon husband Coach Steve spoke highly of me as well.

After Coach made my signing day a success at my high school, I finished preparations that summer for college. I worked at the hospital as a summer job to make some money and that is where I first saw the title 'Physical Therapist.' I was very interested and that would become my intention during my first year of college. Although I only took the required classes to play basketball, I continued to look into different avenues to get into becoming a Licensed Therapist.

I played my first year of college basketball and had a good year playing some varsity and getting an All Star trophy at invitational tournament and tying my high school scoring record of 29 points in a game. I loved to score with the basketball and was never a great shooter but preferred to take the ball to the hole and score with it. I felt I would always get fouled or score or both every time so passing was never on my mind much...

ROUND
5

Robin Rae Redmond

Soon Basketball season was over and I began to go to St. Joseph, Missouri every Wednesday, Friday, and Saturday, as it was the biggest city near the small college I went to. My best friend was a college football player and one night in St. Joseph, he met girl and she had a sister they wanted to introduce me to. Funny, looking back now almost 30 years ago and realizing how much of a miracle it was for Robin Rae to even be back in town at that time as she was living in Florida and happen to be home for a week, which turned into several.

As I'm writing, we will celebrate our twenty-fourth wedding anniversary this July 6th. Chase is 19 years old and Riley Rae is 17 years old. Robin and I are still very much in love.

I've loved Robin since the day we met in 1988 and I know how crazy 'Love at First Sight' sounds but during our first week together, Robin told me, "I LOVE YOU, ROBBIE," leaving me, of course, happy to reply, "I LOVE YOU TOO!"

I finished my first year of college and asked Robin to return to Kentucky with me after we went back to Florida to get all her stuff. Robin and her older sister Lisa had moved to Florida so my cousin David Lunsford and I drove to New Port Richey to pick up my girl who would stay in Kentucky with me until her dad came to get her truck and take her back to St. Joseph so she could help them out at Redmond Produce, the family business.

I loved having her in Kentucky with me, if only for a short time, as she got to see my old high school and we ran around the track that summer. She got to meet my family on both my father's and mother's side and then some of my friends as well as my best friend. Sam called to say he was coming in for weekend from Oklahoma where he went to work with his older brother after high school, so I said, "I will be at your house and I want you to meet my new girlfriend who is beautiful and perfect, Sam, and her name is Robin." He said, "Son of a Bitch, Calloway is in love."

I never realized that would be such a special night. I remember Sam walked up to me when we got there to wrestle but I thought he was giving me a hug because I hadn't seen him in a year so I hugged him and he said, 'Damn you, Calloway, I'm coming up here to toughen you up a little and you're giving me a hug! Robin, Robbie has always been a softie so I don't know what he's told you." We hung out drank a few beers and shared some stories and I told him I'd love for him to look into playing football at Missouri Western and get a college education. He said, "I'm a mechanic, don't you remember how many times I had to fix that piece of junk Camaro of yours or changed your tire?", as he really did; for some reason I never wanted to know anything about fixing cars. I know I'm wrong and wished I had learned or even wanted to learn but always seeing my dad and his brothers outside lying underneath their cars just turned me off. Even as a kid, I said I was going to be the opposite and start my own Calloway name and my kids can learn from my mistakes, as we all make mistakes, but I bet mine won't be as hard to correct. My wife always takes our vehicles to keep serviced so I'm hoping they learn from Robin again as she has always been the best mother to our babies.

I'm thinking of it now so I wanted to put in my story: I believe certain people are just meant to get along due to their birthdays—astronomy—I know it sounds a little weird, but my birthday is July 18th. I love November as Robin's is November 22nd, Chase's November sixth, and Sam was November seventh, Robin's due date for Chase, My baby Riley Rae's birthday is in the summertime like her daddy's, June fourth, and I will always get along with my baby, who I call Butter!!!

I remember my girlfriend enjoying just sitting and talking around the fire with my friends and being able to relax and have a few beers. Robin was always scared she was not going to fit in and I assured her all of my best friends are going to love having her around and they did.

I still feel great that Robin got to meet Sam and I'm glad we gave Chase his name, Chase Samuel Calloway, 11/06/95.

The next day, I took Robin to meet my dad's Mother, Lena, and her mother, Mable, my great grandmother.

I always remember this as I have a photo of the three of them sitting on the couch together and it's so cute. I told Robin to wear her flowery dress when she ask me which one she should wear, so they all three had on very close flowery dresses. Robin looked so damn cute.

When we said goodbye, I felt good that Robin got to meet Sam and Reggie as well as few other friends she had heard me mention. When we loaded up the next day, I talked to her dad, Jerry Redmond, who was called Big Daddy and had driven there to pick up his girl

Robin Rae and take her back to St. Joseph to help out at the produce company. Big Daddy said, "Let's meet up later when you come back to Missouri in a few weeks after you finish your summer job at the hospital."

I'm glad now, but it was hard to let Robin Rae go home with her daddy who was coming through town as he went to get her vehicle in Florida and drove back through Kentucky to pick her up. I remember Big Daddy saying, "Robbie, you finish your job here at the hospital and Robin can work for me at Redmond Produce until you get done and you guys can get back together." Then he said something that we have both repeated over the years, "ABSENCE MAKES THE HEART GROW FONDER."

Of course, I wondered if she would get back to St. Joseph and decide she was not so interested in a guy who was telling her in few years he would have his degree in physical therapy and wanted to talk to her dad about taking him down to register for the Kansas City Golden Gloves because he really thought he could be a good boxer too...

Well Robin did and she loved me as much as I loved her and we began to make our dreams happen together. The best thing was while we were doing it, we had some of the greatest times just cruising around in our car all over town visiting her family and friends and getting to know everything we could about each other.

Robin is very pretty and my family and friends all loved her. I remember my dad's mother saying, "Robbie, does her mom and dad know she is here in Kentucky with you alone?" I said, "Of course, she is older than me, Grandma." She said, "Ok, I love you, but don't start fibbing to your grandma now. I can tell by looking she is just a baby."

One day while I was at Robin's house waiting to return to college the next week for basketball practice, we got a call from my mom. She said, "Robbie, I have some bad news." I said, "What?" She said, "Sam was in a car wreck," so I said, "Is he ok?" She said, "Sam died, Robbie..." I handed the phone to Robin.

We returned to Kentucky for the funeral. I made my mind up I was going to fight for a living on the way back to Missouri from that trip.

I began school at Missouri Western State University in St. Joseph after spending my first year at Tarkio College. I was determined to become a boxer in the Kansas City Golden Gloves as well as stay in college and become a physical therapist. Robin's sister, Toni, was still dating Scott, my friend from college, who introduced Robin and me.

One weekend, we four traveled to Nebraska to watch Scott play a college football game. The girls drove. Scott was on the game bus and planned to meet us back at the dorms.

On the way home, Toni threw an empty can out of the window on our way back and it hit the car behind us. The driver sped up and started yelling to try to pull us over, so I rolled down window. When they saw that I was driving, they sped up and beat us back to the parking lot at the dorms, preparing to kick my ass. The four college football players, who were able to drive back as they were not on the varsity team, recognized me, although I did not know them, and knew I'd be coming back to the college parking lot. I drove up and parked around back as usual and we saw there was already a big crowd of people gathered there, but what we didn't know was that they were there to see these guys kick my ass. I parked the truck and after we rolled down the windows preparing to wait for our friend to get back from the game, the four guys who were in the car behind us came up to the truck, yelling. One reached in and punched me in the face and ripped my shirt before I could get out.

I pushed door open and jumped out and although the other three stood close, the big guy who reached in and threw the punch was the one I wanted to hit back. I started throwing rights and lefts to his face as hard and fast as I could and he began to fall from the blows. He fell into me, grabbing me and taking me to the ground, which was fine with me. He had me on the ground with himself on top but as he was

41

coming for me with his head low, I grabbed under his chin, putting him in a chokehold. Although his buddies were excited, thinking he was on top now and going to kick my ass, they soon saw he was not able to do anything except tap me on the shoulder, begging me to let him up as he could not breathe or speak.

This was in 1988, long before I had ever heard of MMA and before I had ever had my first amateur boxing match. I had several fights coming up and was never afraid to let my hands go, and going to the ground was something I had done as well. I decided to let him up slowly in front of his friends who were all big guys. I was pissed and began yelling to the crowd and to his buddies, "Who wants to step up now?" feeling like I was world champ....

I had blood coming from my chest as he had bit into me on our way to the ground—I still have a scar to this day—but Robin got to see I was a little crazy at times. The next week, Robin Rae told her dad I wanted to go to the Kansas City Golden Gloves and Big Daddy decided he would take me after hearing about the fights from his girls as well as from his friend Herb, whose son Chris told him about seeing me fight one night.

I never thought much about it until writing my book. I don't think I wanted to fight people, but I just did not ever want to be pushed around in any way. I guess I could have just apologized for us throwing the can out the window and hitting their car, but they should have never charged the car and threw the first punch.

FIGHT ME: I MAY HAVE HAD A LITTLE PROBLEM...
SERIOUSLY, OR IS IT JUST ME THINKING THIS...

ROUND
6

Rob and Craig Cummings

Amateur Boxing

Big Daddy took me to Whatsoever Boxing Club in Kansas City to begin my boxing career. I helped out at Redmond Produce, unloading trucks on weekends, and each day after college, I drove to Kansas City to Whatsoever to train and spar with whomever I could. Soon it was time for the Kansas City Golden Glove tournament. Big Daddy took me to my first fight only a couple weeks after I had started training. The age divisions were 17-20 and 21 and over. I was 19 at the time and my opponent was in his early 20s and had just over 20 fights, but I wanted the fight so Big Daddy said we would take it. Well, it was a tough 3-round victory by decision. I was so happy and Big Daddy was proud and happy as well. The next day he called and said, "Rob, bring that trophy over here to the bar." He would always go to the Shotz Tavern on Frederick to unwind, as he called it. Then we drove to few more spots he had some friends at, including the card shop at Herb Moore's place, Big Daddy's best friend who had a poker room for years.

Herb had said to me. "If Jerry don't take you down to the Kansas City Golden Gloves, I will" as his son Chris had told him I was a fighter. One day he had stopped his car as I was fighting on the ground with one of the guys and the other who was his friend was getting ready to get involved as well. While driving by, Chris saw something going on and said, "Hey, only one on one." I always liked Chris and respected him for that. He was the drummer in *Charlie and the Sting Rays* who were a great local band in St. Joseph, Missouri.

Big Daddy got VCR tapes of a trainer in Texas he liked and he would have me following his running routine each morning. I remember our first National Golden Gloves when we had an opportunity to meet coach Kenny Weldon and it meant a lot to Big Daddy and myself. We spoke about how impressed he was that I was even at the Nationals with only seven amateur bouts under my belt. We also got to see Joe Frazier's son and many of the other boxing people. I loved just

45

being in the company of so many other young men who had the same aspirations as I did and I still remember some legendary fighters who were introduced prior to opening bell, including Jake Lamotta and Gene Fullmer. My father-in-law loved getting to see them even if from a distance. I thought that is what I want—to be respected by lots of people for being able to fight really well and maybe even one day, having people like Big Daddy stand up and clap for me just for being introduced.

We lived on Jackson Street for a year then moved to a little house on Edmond Street in St. Joseph then to a smaller town 12 miles south of St. Joseph closer to Kansas City as I would be driving to KC daily for college therapy program. This was our home when we got married on July 6th, 1991 after dating over 3 years. It made it an easier drive for me, as I would go to work out at the boxing gym after college.

We leased a beautiful stucco duplex on Noyes Boulevard for a year while I drove about a mile and a half to work at the Sports Rehabilitation Clinic on Frederick Avenue. I did one of my last clinicals for school there and met John Gillaspie. Soon after, Robin and I bought our first home in midtown St. Joseph, Missouri just down the street from the little house we had rented together for over a year.

I had a great amateur career, although starting late at 19-years-old, I was able to win the Most Outstanding Boxer in the Kansas City Golden Gloves and won by knockout in the finals against Darrin Crowder. In the semifinals, I had to face a fighter who I had lost to in both the finals of the Joplin Golden Gloves as well as the Springfield Golden Gloves, but each fight was close and with Crowder having 175 amateur bouts and me going the distance both times in only my second and third amateur fights ever, my father-in-law had a feeling I had a special future in the sport of boxing. I was just thinking about winning the next bout. I won the decision versus Crowder in our third fight as well as giving him a standing eight in the third round. I was very

46

happy with the win, as was my father-in-law, Big Daddy. He was just happy I was able to give him such a great fight in our first two bouts, but I really thought I was going to win and did.

I won the KC Open Division the next year, beating several fighters along the way from preliminaries to quarterfinals to semifinals to finals and each were older with more experience than me. The man I beat in the championship had been a KC Golden Gloves champion several years, but I won by boxing aggressively and earning my way to Des Moines, Iowa for a chance at the National Golden Gloves. I lost that decision in the quarterfinals of the National Golden Gloves, but I remember all the great fighters who were present and how fun it was for me and my father-in-law to be right in the middle of all the great amateurs from around the country.

I won the Missouri State Championship almost one year prior to the Olympic Trials for 1992 in St. Louis. I fought Jimmy Compton and this would be one of my best victories as an amateur. Big Daddy and I went to St. Louis for the State Title and what an amateur fight we had. Jimmy Compton was ranked #3 in the USA behind Jeremy Williams and John Ruiz who went on to become the Heavyweight Champion. I remember feeling like I did in several of my 12-round fights as a professional, as we battled all 3 rounds with me winning a unanimous decision, making Big Daddy very proud.

A few months later, I fought a guy from Kansas City who I had beaten a several weeks earlier by knockout. I learned a very valuable lesson, as it would be the first time I would take training lightly. I don't remember any sparring before the match. I lost a 3-round decision, which I still think I won as I feel I landed more shots and cleaner, more effective punches, but instead of focusing on that, I want to say congratulations to Mark Cipolla for doing what it took to win. Congratulations, Champ. I learned a valuable lesson and realized not to let a bout become close when you're fighting a KC fighter from a KC club or really anybody.

I went on to St. Louis to beat fighters, earning my way to USA's and Olympic Trials. I had a great time going with my father-in-law,

Jerry Big Daddy Redmond, to Fort Huachuca in Arizona, south of Phoenix and fighting my way to the semifinals where I lost a fair decision to the first southpaw I faced as an amateur. He lost in the finals to Jeremy Williams, who I had heard of for years as an amateur and always liked and respected but also always wanted to fight as an amateur. It was probably a good thing I didn't because Jeremy was a very good amateur boxer who could really punch well.

On the long trip home, I spoke with my father-in-law and decided the best way to turn professional was to sign with Peyton Sher from Kansas City for whom we had our first professional fight October of 1992 in Wichita Kansas.

Peyton Sher was the matchmaker for Don King. My friend and groomsmen at Robin's and my wedding, Craig Cummings, was also under contract with Peyton. Craig's dad, Tom Cummings, even agreed to help out as trainer in my corner as he and my father-in-law were best friends. Tom was my coach through the remainder of my amateur career after leaving the Whatsoever Gym with Coach Steve Leon. Steve was a great coach and good friend, but my father-in-law wanted me to go with Tom to Kansas City Missouri Recreation and I feel it was great move for me as well.

Tom had spoken to my father-in-law and me about letting Steve Homan, a Kansas City Lightweight who was a very good amateur from Kansas City and had a good professional career as well, become my head coach. Steve was a good boxer and I am still happy we went with Steve as he showed me how to box, using my jab, bringing the right hand, and finishing with a hook. This may sound pretty simple but I really thank him for the drives from Lee Summit to St. Joseph, Missouri after he got off work for years to train me. His holding the mitts and movements were beneficial to me and he helped me during the beginning up until we fought for our first professional world title in Boise, Idaho versus Cruiserweight Champion, Kenny Keene. I was a fan of Kenny's and he was nice enough to call me on a couple of occasions to congratulate me after some of my big wins after our bout.

I was very proud and happy to have a great boxer like Craig

Cummings call me up throughout my career after I won a big fight on TV and very proud that he was able to stand up with me for Robin's and my wedding.

ROUND 7

The summer of 1991, I married my best friend, Robin Rae Redmond.

The greatest WIN in my 132-fight career was when Robin Rae Redmond said yes to my proposal of marriage at the Red Lobster in St. Joseph, Missouri just 6 months after we had met.

I bought her an engagement ring my last semester in Tarkio from a girl's grandmother. That girl is a friend to Robin and me to this day. We recently went to her church as she had asked me to be a speaking guest. Robin loved that little engagement ring and was sweet enough to wear it with pride for me. Her dad and mom acted as if they loved it too, however when Big Daddy got the first chance, he said, "I have a friend, Harry Heitman, who owns a jewelry shop downtown. I will take you down to see if you can get Robin a bigger ring and you can pay me back when you can." I loved him for this and I know he just wanted his daughter to have a beautiful ring, which she got.

We had a beautiful wedding on July 6, 1991 at Wyatt Park Baptist Church and a beautiful poolside reception at her mom and dad's home, a little over three years later after I had graduated college. I had been working in physical therapy for Charlie Edwards at the St. Joseph Physical Therapy and Sports Rehabilitation Clinic since May 1991.

I was still an amateur boxer and won the Kansas City Golden Gloves again and went to the 1992 USA Olympic Trials in Ft Huachuca, Arizona after winning our Regionals in St. Louis. I lost in the semifinals of the western trials and afterwards was offered the opportunity to go professional with Peyton Sher, who was also managing Craig Cummings, my friend and one of the groomsmen at our wedding. Robin was beautiful and still looks the same.

Robin had her sister Toni as Maid of Honor, and Lori Hill, Lori Norton, Crystal Lankford—girlfriends from High school—and her oldest sister, Julie Bielby—my favorite, who looks so much like my beautiful wife, Robin—all stand up with her as Maids of Honor. Martin and Julie's daughter Jazity was our flower girl, my sister's two little boys, Josh and Bryan, were our ring bearers, and I had Jon Koelliker as my best man, Craig Cummings, Martin Bielby, Bill Eaton, and Scott Zeus, stand up with me as groomsmen.

I was living a dream, having a respectful job with college degree and pursuing my boxing dream as professional. In October of 1992, I had my first professional bout in Wichita, Kansas. I had a few months off between my loss in the Olympic Trials in Arizona and my first professional fight in Wichita. My amateur trainer, Tom Cummings, introduced me to Steve Homan who was a former professional fighter and was a lightweight who did well as a local professional. He was good for me at that time of my career and I will always thank 'The Hammer' Steve Homan for his help in the corner.

Robin and I dated over three years and were married over three years before having children, so we became best friends and enjoyed the same things, even high school sports. She liked coming along to see the local high schools play and we would always cheer for her alma mater, Benton, until her brother began playing for the Central Indians of which we became fans. I remember saying their 1995 team was the best football team I had ever personally seen in high school. I also became a fan of Coach Dudik and I remember late in his career at Central, he and I were speaking one night at a high school event. He asked me about my thoughts of Bishop Leblond High School and I only remember saying I never considered sending Chase there, as we are not Catholic. He did not mention we could still go to high school there and if he had, I may have talked Chase into going to Leblond to play football for him. I still thought Central was where Chase would be going, however, as Coleman Elementary School, then Bode Middle School led to Central High, but I learned there were several before us who would choose different high schools to attend as it was allowed by the city as long as transportation was provided.

I believe many things happen for reasons unknown such as why we had our kids go to Lafayette High School in the first place, as we were in Central's school district, and with Robin being a Benton graduate, if we were not going to attend Central high school, we should have at least looked into Benton High but…

We did not and I was Lil Krazy around this time anyway with my boxing career coming to an end and although many believe I had a successful career, I did not make the money I should have made. I HAVE TO LIVE WITH THAT and I have now become at peace with myself and understand I did the best I could do in every fight I had...PERIOD.

Unfortunately OR Fortunately, many got to see me going through much of my craziness, as I would post on Facebook. Although I drove some closest to me crazy, they saw how much I loved them.

Just many times certain things happen at certain times and for whatever reason it was not meant to be. Right, I don't know what I'm saying either, but I've learn to live with myself, accepting that some paths in our life we cross, or at times in our life when we're asked to fight through, to get to the better, more peaceful side are just tests GOD is giving us. I always say I know what's right and wrong and I believe I have been given so many favors from GOD for making the right choices along my many tough paths in life, I'll just keep trying to fight through. 45 years old right now...

I HAVE TO SAY THANK GOD FOR SENDING ROBIN RAE REDMOND HOME TO ST JOSEPH, MISSOURI IN 1988, ALLOW-ING ME TO MEET HER AND FOR US BOTH TO FALL IN LOVE, AS I CANNOT IMAGINE LIFE WITHOUT HER OR WHERE MY LIFE WOULD HAVE LED ME IF NOT FOR ROBIN RAE CAL-LOWAY!!!!

I had taken a job at St. Joseph Physical Therapy and Sports Reha-bilitation Clinic and we bought our first home on Edmond Street a year later, close to Central High School where Robin would spend many days walking around the track.

I always think about how blessed I was to have an opportunity to do a six-week clinical at the Sports Rehabilitation Clinic in St. Joseph and meet Charlie Edwards, the owner, and John Gillaspie, a RPT who was a very good athlete as well who ran track at Kansas State University. He and his wife, Dottie, became good friends to me as well as to Robin. John became my best friend for many years and helped me in physical therapy, telling me to save money and buy stocks; he helped us with intelligent information on buying our first, second, and third house, which is the house we're in at this time still after 14 years. John was always helpful and we really became great friends.

I took Robin and the kids to Disney World in Florida one time after one of my first big fights and John and Dottie came to Kentucky to pick us up and meet my family, as we flew from Florida to Kentucky for a visit as well. GOD takes the best people away from us at times without us ever knowing why. John said he thought he had hemorrhoids and was getting it checked out when we returned from Kentucky, but it was colon cancer and I lost another great friend who will never be replaced. I'm glad he got to see our children and I'm glad I got to spend so many great days and nights with my friend John. He took me to Kansas State Football games as he had season tickets since he was an All-American in track for them and remained a big K-State fan.

We also liked country music so we spent many nights hanging out. We may have been able to start a country group… well, never mind, we only sounded good to ourselves, Robin and Dottie finally told us.

DAMN RIGHT I LIKE THE LIFE I LIVE BECAUSE I WENT FROM NEGATIVE TO POSITIVE…

I felt so great with my beautiful wife Robin Rae as we bought our first house and I was working at the Physical Therapy and Sports Rehabilitation Clinic in St. Joseph for two great guys, Charlie and John, as well as another Physical Therapist, Amy Cole, who was a very nice young lady. I just remember learning so much from each of them but the most important thing I learned was to be a good person, care about people, and enjoy the fact we were blessed enough to help people rehabilitate from sport or work injuries. I learned so many valuable lessons in-patient care from the three of them and I hope I told each of them enough how much I cared for them and appreciated them. I was honored and proud John asked to carry one of my belts out for a fight in my career up in Iowa, as he usually just sat ringside with his wife and Robin, but that time he went out of town with me and my whole team and we had a great time celebrating the fourth-round knockout later at the after-fight party. I love and miss John often and he will never be forgotten.

ROUND
8

FIGHT #1
1992-10-24 Kenny Brown, Wichita, Kansas, USA W 4

I remember being excited to become a pro boxer under contract with Peyton Sher, who was a matchmaker for Don King. I really thought I was on my way with my family all driving over with some close friends to see my first professional boxing match. I won all four rounds by listening to my coach, Steve Homan, and using my jab, out-pointing my opponent fairly easily without taking any unnecessary risks. One of the trainers in our locker room said, "Calloway must not be a big puncher, as I thought he would have stopped that guy." I have a problem with anything negative said about me. It bothers me even though who gives a damn what some guy thought or said. But I never quite seem to be able to ignore people and even late in my career, people's words would hurt my feelings and make me fight better so I guess I should say thanks to my critics. I didn't remember I was fighting for money in my first fight until we were on our way home after Big Daddy asked if I got my check. He had good laugh when I got nervous and said, "Go back. I really forgot I was fighting for money now." He reached in his pocket and pulled out the check.

I said, "Pull over when we get to a restaurant. I'm buying." Big Daddy laughed and said, "I guess I can loan you some if you're paying for us all." He was the one who got my check for me so he knew how much it was for.

FIGHT #2
1993-01-17 Ron Jackson, Hyatt Regency Ballroom, Saint Louis, Missouri, USA W KO 1

Three months later, we were asked to fight in St. Louis and we had a great time driving to the fight in Big Daddy's Lincoln Town Car, staying in a nice hotel. This time Big Daddy did not have to pay for it as he always had throughout my amateur career as well as all the food and drink. Many times, he paid for the whole amateur team, not just for me, as Jerry 'Big Daddy' Redmond really liked and respected the sport of boxing. I'm glad he and I got to spend so much time together, letting me realize years later it's all those little things and times together that were the most fun and the ones my memory remains so fond of.

FIGHT #3
1993-05-06 Aaron Platt, St. Louis, Missouri, USA W KO 1

Four months later, we were asked to return to St. Louis and I began to really like the trips and began to realize although I was not making a lot of money, the fact it was not costing my father-in-law to drive and put us up for the night in a hotel as well as feed us, not to mention all the boxing equipment he always paid for, but now I was getting room free and paid to fight made it a little less expensive on Big Daddy. He never complained and I know he loved me like one of his own. I remember this fight as it was versus an opponent from Cleveland and I landed one of my best right hands to knock him out in the first round. I was able to keep getting little better each fight, learning things like getting the correct distance to set up the punch I was planning to throw and from the correct angle. I remember the St. Louis crowd really liked the overhand right I threw and the knockout was a beautiful punch. Big Daddy and I were on our way to the Lincoln Town Car after the bout and one of the spectators said, "Hey Calloway, if you ever hit somebody like that again here in St. Louis, we are going to have you arrested!" I think Big Daddy liked the comment more than me.

FIGHT #4
1993-06-25 Rodney Coe, Saint Louis, Missouri, USA W 4

A month later, we were asked to return to the same venue in St. Louis as I was beginning to get a small following from the St. Louis area, who were all great boxing fans. I would win every round versus Coe who was a former Missouri football player and a strong guy. I just boxed from the outside as instructed by my trainer, Steve Homan, who was a good boxing lightweight as professional himself few years before. I was able to drop Coe with a body punch close to the end of the round, but I give him credit for getting up and finishing the fight.

This would be our last fight in St. Louis for a while. The next morning at the hotel, we all went to breakfast and Big Daddy asked the waitress, "Do you have pancakes?" and she said, "Yes, Sir" and then went on to take everyone else's orders. She was getting ready to leave for the kitchen and Big Daddy said, "Ain't you forgetting someone?" She said, "Your pancakes will be up shortly." Big Daddy said I just asked if you were serving them, I didn't know I ordered any yet." , as he was always in a mess and usually with lunch ladies for some reason. I think Jason, Robin's younger brother, loved that and probably remembers things like this the most as he went along with us to many bouts and would always video tape them on the camcorder. GREAT TIMES!

FIGHT #5
1993-08-23 Larry McFadden, Civic Arena, Saint Joseph, Missouri, USA W KO 1

My first bout at the St. Joseph Civic Arena was against Larry 'Black Magic' McFadden, August 23rd 1993. I knocked him out with a left hook, leading to many bouts at the Civic to follow. I remember a patient from the Sports Rehab Clinic saying, "You mean that little punch you hit him with knocked him out? I saw it on the news." I said, "It sure did. What do you mean anyway?" and he said, "Well that little punch didn't seem like enough to knock anyone out." I began to realize I was never going to be able to please or impress everyone from our hometown with my boxing. I said, "How about you or someone you feel confident could beat me come down to my boxing gym and spar with me and see if anyone can go longer than that professional boxer was able to go." I willing to bet $100 they wouldn't last three minutes, as that is a long time in the ring. Well, he brought his younger brother down who was in his 20's. I was 23 at the time and after about 30-45 seconds, he wanted to quit. When you're in the boxing ring with a man who is going to beat you in the head and has the ability to knock you unconscious like you've seen him do before on TV, all the questions you have asked yourself that nobody knows about except you are going through your mind again, only now in front of your big brother who is going to tell everyone in your family what happened. You don't know, but I do: he is thanking GOD he is not the one in the ring so you will not see the coward he is by quitting sooner than you did after I hit him in the head, then as he gets tired and all those questions you're asking yourself right now, he would not have the answers for either, which would make him quit...

The man pulled out $100 to pay, as I actually forgot the bet, but I said, "Keep the money and just come to watch me fight at the Civic when you get a chance." He said, "We absolutely will, Rob, and we'll bring more people too.

I realized working in the Physical Therapy and Sports Rehabilitation Clinic of St. Joseph, helping patients rehabilitate from injury was where I actually spoke to many local residents on a daily basis. They would go home and tell whomever they spoke to about talking to this therapist who is a boxer as well and trains here in St. Joseph and married Robin Redmond from Benton High School. I had many men that would come down to see my father-in-law and tell him Rob ask me to come down to see the gym. Of course, my father-in-law was a lot like me—or me like him—but we both knew we needed sparring and wanted to show everyone why we had to go to Kansas City to even get anyone to get into the ring with me to spar. So Big Daddy always asked if they would like to get in the ring and spar a couple rounds, letting them know he had large sparring gloves and headgear for them to wear as well. This went on for several years as the word got around town and soon to all the right people who if they did not feel confident in themselves enough, had a friend or knew of someone who would like to get in the ring and fight a few rounds with me. One round is three minutes and I don't think there was anyone who went four-three minute rounds with me and most never finished the first or second round. There were other professional boxers, of course, that we would arrange to have come up at times, but there was never a person who was not a very skilled amateur or professional boxer who was able to spar with me more than two rounds, usually one, as I never let anyone gain too much confidence. I always thought after they leave it would be easy for them to begin to make themselves believe they did better than they actually was able to do.

My father-in-law loved the way I felt about sparring and he felt the same way I did. We didn't go easy in sparring. Go ahead and bring it and if you get hit too hard or knocked down, then of course we'll stop and wait until your head clears up. If you want to continue, then we can continue, but absolutely if you bring it hard for a minute and a half then quit when there is minute and a half still remaining, then that's not acceptable. Finish the round. Get knocked out or quit. I always hated anyone who would think they were going to bring it 30 seconds and land a few punches then quit. They better run and jump out of the ring if sparring with me. I made it clear always we were sparring three-three minute rounds unless you knock me out or I knock you out. I won't quit so you won't either from fatigue, only after you've taken a beating, or you give me a beating.

NEVER HAPPENED....

FIGHT #6
1993-10-23 Ken McCurdy, Civic Arena, Saint Joseph, Missouri, USA L SD 6

My next bout was against Ken McCurdy and although I scored a clean knockdown, it was called a slip and he would win by split decision. It was a fight I always regretted as I thought I clearly won, but it seldom was ever talked about, as only a few knew who I even was at the time. The next few bouts would see me improve and I began to fight with more aggression. Steve was a boxing lightweight and continued to want me to use my jab. I think he was good for me at that time of my career.

FIGHT #7
1994-02-10 Willie Jackson, Civic Arena, Saint Joseph, Missouri, USA W KO 1

I fought February 10, 1994 again at the Civic Arena winning by a first round knockout. Jackson was a little light heavyweight and I was still pissed about my last fight, so brought everything I could early and got him out of there in the first round.

I'm not sure if it was this bout in particular, but I remember my friend Craig Cummings being the Main Event and our Manager/Promoter at the time, Peyton Sher, bringing in Frankie Randall to fight on the card and spar with Craig. I also remember Bones Adams coming in as well on occasion. My father-in-law really loved Bones and he came to his house with all of us. We swam in the pool and had a great time with us each sharing our dreams. Now looking back, it's great to see that Bad Bones Adams got to live and fulfill his dreams just as I did, especially knowing we are both from Kentucky, originally anyway.

I remember watching Bones sparring with Ricardo Cepeda who was a great fighter from the Bronx by way of Puerto Rico. I think Cepeda fought for the world title but was never able to capture the crown. Bones did and I will always be thankful we became friends. I've loved watching his career and hope he got to see mine go a long way as well. I remember we visited him when my father- and mother-in-law went to Kentucky with us to visit my family. We stopped to see Bones and his family as my mother-in-law loved Bad Bones very much just like everybody, I guess, including Robin and me. I remember him getting to see Chase and I know Bones would love to see Chase nowadays and see what a great young man and fighter he has become.

I remember Frankie 'The Surgeon' Randall winning impressively but most of all, I remember Frankie being a great guy who I thought would be a great trainer one day as he showed me some things I had never been taught before. We were only together a couple of days, but as it was very early in my career, I remember just him coaching me in the gym with a jumping rope and hitting the heavy bag, sometimes all hard straight punches and sometimes boxing and burning out in the last 30 seconds. He was a great guy and a great fighter and I hope he is well. I remember Frankie telling me he wanted to fight Julio Cesar Chavez and I was thinking "WHY?" No one could beat that guy as Chavez was around 80-0 at that time. Robin, Big Daddy, Ilene, and I always spent the weekend watching him fight and win every chance we got.

But Frankie 'The Surgeon' Randall said, "I can beat him, Rob." WOW. I love to tell that story as couple years later, he sure did. I hope the Champ and one of the Best Pound-for-Pound fighters I ever met— Frankie 'The Surgeon' Randall—is well. GOD bless you, Champ!

I'm writing my book and thinking again how lucky I was to meet my wife Robin Rae and how blessed I was that her dad and I loved each other so much. I know my boxing career was good for me, but I realize now how good it was for my father-in-law as well. I think he enjoyed and needed being a part of the fight game and I hope he loved it the last several years of his life as much as I did. I remember he always enjoyed meeting the fighters just like I still do. One of my favorites at that time was Alex Stewart. He fought Evander Holyfield twice with the first being a very good fight, and he also fought Iron Mike Tyson. I remember Alex telling me, "Rob, the amateurs are the best for experience" as Alex was a good amateur prior to becoming a great professional. I also remember him telling me, "Rob, always pay your taxes as boxing money will add up. We are paid in spurts, so try to pay after each fight so you don't find yourself having to pay too much in one lump sum." I'm sorry, Robin Rae Calloway, I did not always listen to the good advice I was given all those years I love you though...

FIGHT #8
1994-04-21 Derrick Edwards, Las Vegas, Nevada, USA
W KO 2

I was asked to come to Las Vegas for my next bout on April 21, 1994. I fought a house fighter from Jamaica at the Silver Nugget, Derrick Edwards. I was tall for a Light Heavyweight, standing 6'2½", but Edwards, living and training in Las Vegas, trying to make a career of the sport, was 2-3 inches taller than me. However, he was 'Too Thin to Win' and had 'Not Enough Ass to Last.' I knocked him out in the second round and it was a great trip to Las Vegas for me and Robin as well as her dad and the rest of our team.

I remember being a fan of James 'Lights Out' Toney. He was a guest that night and I was glad I got to meet him prior to the fight as well as afterwards when we got to speak a little.

Much later in my career, I was offered a fight with James. I took the bout and went to training camp until we got a call saying he would be fighting Hasim 'Rock' Rahman instead. I was a fan of James my entire career, however, I became friends with Rock much later in my career after our fight in 2002. But I always thought James was one of the best fighters pound-for-pound his entire career. He and Rock fought to a 10 round draw.

Once I got back to St. Joseph to work at the sports rehab clinic, we had a patient who I had met at the YMCA while in the hot tub after Big Daddy had me on the track doing our running routine. David and I began to talk and he was so excited when I told him I was from Kentucky and lived in Louisville and was there when Ali regained the World Title. I told him that was my earliest memory and one of the reasons I've always loved the sport of boxing, that everyone respected Ali for fighting. We even spoke about Greg Page and he knew who he was and was a fan as well, so I knew David was a true boxing fan. He told me of his amateur days on the south side of Louisville, going to the gym and he loved hearing my story. David Lee Reynolds was one of my best friends from that moment on. He loved and supported me my entire career. I loved him as well. I'll speak of David much more along my boxing life as well as life in general, as we became friends for years to come. RIP Champ!

FIGHT #9
1994-05-25 Carlos Vasquez, Civic Arena, Saint Joseph, Missouri, USA W KO 5

Lito and I had a good fight. I had heard of him but never sparred him but was told he was from the Army and fought in the service and had some amateur experience as well as ability to punch with his right hand pretty well. I was beginning to gain some fans and this was a good bout for me as people could see he was a good-looking fighter with a built physique. He really brought the fight to me and soon I took over with my power jab right hand, finishing with left hook and was able to continue with pressure until landing some big shots that led the ref to step in and stop the fight in the fifth round. Lito was living in Kansas City then and I figured we would fight again one day. We did almost exactly a year later in Kansas City.

FIGHT #10
1994-08-25 Roman Santos, Las Vegas, Nevada, USA
L PTS 5

Changed from 8 to 5 rounder. We had never heard of it either, but we made it happen.

First broken hand… We soon got another call to fight again in Las Vegas versus another hometown fighter, Roman Santos. I lost in a decision to him. I wish I had been more aggressive, however, with Steve my boxing coach, we again chose to box, letting Santos be the aggressor in his home town, making it an easy decision for the judges. I also broke my right hand, which made it tougher to be more aggressive. I was never real close to Steve. He had 'little man' disease, I guess. He was a lightweight and a real good boxer. I felt he was always jealous of Tony Chiaverini who was more liked in our area and even landed a fight with one of the greatest of all time: Sugar Ray Leonard. Steve had a lot of problems and I really just wish him the best in his life. I know I came a lot farther than he ever thought I could come in the sport of boxing, and I hope he has had a chance to see some of my fights on television and wins on ESPN in the heavyweight division.

Whatever—it is what it is and was what it was. Good luck to you, Steve.

I give Steve credit for driving up from Lee Summit to St. Joseph to train me prior to fights and we went down to his house for some big fights at times. I considered us friends, and nothing has changed that. I won't discuss it, but he was going through a lot of stuff with his home life and even brought trouble to camp. For example, once in Vegas prior to my world title fight in Boise Idaho, which everyone knows is wrong, but I also disagreed with his training style and some of his beliefs. Although I went along with it until losing the decision for the world title, and I told my manager I did not feel comfortable with

Steve as head coach anymore and wanted a change. I feel that I have proved I was right by not only coming further than he thought possible, but became a good heavyweight champion by winning ESPN's Fight of the Year in Australia and also by winning big fights on television that I know he got to see. I hope he feels good he was first professional boxing coach and kept me sharp for several years.

FIGHT #11
1995-02-13 Kevin Cloughlay, Marriott Allis Plaza Hotel, Kansas City, Missouri, USA W KO 4

Our next bout was back in Kansas City, downtown at the Allis Plaza. I won by KO against my first kickboxer who got in the ring to make some cash as a boxer as well.

Cloughlay had some kickboxing fans he brought to the fight so it was good for me to beat a local KC fighter in front of his crowd. I controlled each round behind my jab, aggressively followed by my right hand and hook until winning by KO in round four.

One of the best things about this fight was that the ring announcer was the legendary Michael Buffer who always said, "LET'S GET READY TO RUMBLE..."

Robin and I had married three and a half years earlier and after trips to California for continuing education courses as well as a very special honeymoon to San Francisco, California and me fighting in Las Vegas twice, we began to plan for having our first baby. Robin was a great expectant mother. I'll never forget her coming home from the doctor's office the day she was supposed to find out if she was pregnant. I said, "So are you?" and she said, "I'm not for sure still. "

I loved working in Physical Therapy at the Sports Rehabilitation Clinic and Charlie was great about sending me for continuing education so I could be educated on some of the machines we used for testing at the clinic such as the BTE, CYBEX, and some work-hardening tools. One of my first clinics was held in Orlando so after I was told I would be going, I made plans for Robin and I to make a vacation out of it as well. I finished my couple days of work then Robin and I spent the next week on CoCo Beach.

THE EXCITING THING ABOUT THIS TRIP WAS A FEW HOURS BEFORE WE LEFT, ROBIN HAD HER CHECK-UP AS WE HAD BEEN TRYING TO HAVE OUR FIRST BABY. WE HAD BEEN PRACTICING FOR YEARS.... SO THAT EXPLAINS WHY SHE GAVE BIRTH TO THE CHAMP 9 MONTHS LATER... I'LL NEVER FORGET MY BEAUTIFUL WIFE TELLING ME WHEN I ASKED, "WHAT DID THE DOCTOR HAVE TO SAY?" SHE SAID, "WELL I'M NOT POSITIVE." I SAID, "WHAT DO YOU MEAN YOU'RE NOT POSITIVE—ARE YOU PREGNANT OR NOT?" SHE SAID, "DOCTOR CORDER NEVER SAID I WAS PREGNANT. HE JUST TOLD ME THE DUE DATE WAS NO-VEMBER SEVENTH BUT NEVER REALLY SAID, 'ROBIN, YOU'RE PREGNANT." I SAID, "OMG! YES YES YES AWE-SOME! THEN WE'RE HAVING A BABY!!!!!!!" WELL ROBIN WAS A PERFECT MOMMY-TO-BE. OF COURSE SHE SWAM IN THE OCEAN THE WHOLE TIME WE IN FLORIDA. SHE NEVER SHOWED A TUMMY AT ALL UNTIL WE GOT HOME FROM VACATION AS SHE WORE TWO-PIECE ON BEACH. AFTER RETURNING HOME, I BOUGHT SOME NON-ALCOHOLIC CHAMPAGNE TO CELEBRATE AND SHE WOULD NOT EVEN TASTE IT BECAUSE IT SAID 'CHAMPAGNE.' I SAID, "NO AL-COHOL" AND SHE CRIED AND SAID, "I DON'T WANT TO EVEN TASTE IT CAUSE I ONLY WANT BABY TO HAVE ALL HEALTHY STUFF FROM FIRST MINUTE." I LOVE HER SO MUCH FOR THAT; SHE ALWAYS PUT HER BABIES BEFORE HERSELF EVER SINCE THAT DAY. WELL, I LOVE ALL THREE OF THEM MORE THAN ANYTHING, BUT I DRANK THE NON-ALCOHOLIC CHAMPAGNE THEN HIT THE HARD STUFF TO CELEBRATE ALONE.

FIGHT #12
1995-05-11 Carlos Vasquez, Marriott Allis Plaza Hotel, Kansas City, Missouri, USA W KO 3

My fight with Carlito Vasquez, our second as I had beat him by TKO almost a year earlier in St. Joseph, was one with excitement as after the 2nd round I returned to the corner and told Big Daddy, "Don't take my mouthpiece out. My jaw's broken." He said, "What the hell is wrong?" I said, "I'm gonna knock him out" and he said, "Well, you got one round or I'm gonna stop it." I was very aggressive and landed some big shots and was able to stop Lito that next round. We celebrated with the crowd until we got back to the locker room and Big Daddy noticed my cheekbone was indented. Lito had landed an overhand right that broke my zygomatic arch (cheekbone) and I guess proved again to Big Daddy and to some others that heard about the fight afterwards that I was either a little crazy or was willing to win no matter what. I wanted to be the best around Kansas City and the Midwest but I also already had plans and dreams of one day fighting and winning a world title.

Robin and I loved our little house on Edmond street but I was ready to get us a bigger house after finding out Robin was having baby and my boxing was getting better. Most of all, I had great job in physical therapy at the Sports Rehab Clinic, which I loved very much as well.

FIGHT #13
1995-08-26 Vance Winn, Argosy Riverboat, Kansas City, Missouri, USA W UD 6

Three months later I was back in the ring again after healing up from the broken zygomatic arch. I fought aggressively and Vance battled right back, however, I felt my power as after three rounds of getting rocked, he stopped being aggressive and was willing to just survive with me and take a decision loss. I didn't let him know—or at least tried to hide as much as I could—that I broke my right hand on his skull. I continued to be aggressive but mainly using my left jab and hook as it began to hurt every time I landed my right. This was the second time I broke my hand and I was coming off a broken cheekbone in the fight before this one. I began to rethink if this is what I wanted to do. The broken hand came almost exactly a year to the day I had broke it the first time in Vegas.

Robin Rae was expecting our son Chase Samuel Calloway to be born in early November so I decided not to fight anymore until after he was born. Robin and I began to go to Lamaze classes, which was something that was good for us just to be together and learn more about how our baby was growing and what to expect in a few months.

We continued to drive around looking at open houses each weekend until soon the realtor helping us asked if we would be interested in making a trade with a young lady who was going through a divorce. The realtor looked through our home on Edmond and said it just might work out for her. Julie came to check everything out and decided it would work well as she also had a daycare. We knew her house on Robin Lane would be perfect for us at the time with us now preparing to start our family and we just loved the neighborhood. The deal was made and we lived there for seven years raising our babies there with Chase going to kindergarten, catching the bus each day walking down the hill like a little man. Robin told Julie she was interested in bringing Chase to her house for daycare as well after the deal was complete. Robin and I loved Julie as she had several little kids and always did great with introducing Chase to schoolwork. It was great for him to be around other little kids as well and soon as Riley Rae was old enough to begin, she was so excited to join as well. I think Robin cried every day the first few months of both daycare and kindergarten. I know she loved Julie as well as our kids' kindergarten teachers, but I guess that is the difference in Mom and Dad. Maybe that is why the kids love Robin more than me? OK joking…they have to tell us they love us the same.

Lamaze classes was something we began to look forward to each week and after seeing one of Robin's girlfriends from the neighborhood was in the class as well made it even more fun for us. Christine's husband Pat was a friend of mine as well. I really had not had a chance to meet him yet but had seen him around town with Christine's brothers who Robin had known since kids so I felt like I was friends with them as well.

We loved going to class and would one day get together with the babies and take pictures, loving every minute of it. Many years later after going our separate ways and being in our busy lives, we ended up living only a block away from each other in Carriage Oaks. They had a beautiful baby girl, Carleigh, born October 7th, who I like to say was Chase's first girlfriend. When they would come over when Chase and Carleigh were beautiful little babies, we would take pictures of them sitting up on our couch together. I'm so happy to say they are still friends to this day even though going to different high schools. Carleigh is a great swimmer and goes to Central High School.

OUR SON CHASE SAMUEL CALLOWAY WAS BORN
11/06/95—GREATEST DAY OF MY LIFE.

Robin had a perfect pregnancy and at the last checkup, the doctor said, "Keep an eye on her blood pressure as its getting high and if it continues or gets higher, go ahead and bring her in." I checked each day several times and one day I called John and Dotty and had them come over to check. They thought we should go on in to the hospital and Robin started crying as I did as well. Robin was admitted and they tried to induce to let her have the baby naturally but when the baby's heart rate started to be too low to hear, they rushed in after hours of labor and took Robin to the delivery room fast. I love each of the nurses and Dr. Robert Corder so much for saving my beautiful wife and our perfect son Chase born in just few minutes via C-Section and that was the happiest day of my life up to that point as Robin was so happy and healthy and we had a beautiful 8-pound son, Chase Samuel Calloway. Chase was 7 lb 15 oz and 21½ inches long to be exact, which was the same as his daddy. I was so proud of that Lil Champ. Beautiful.

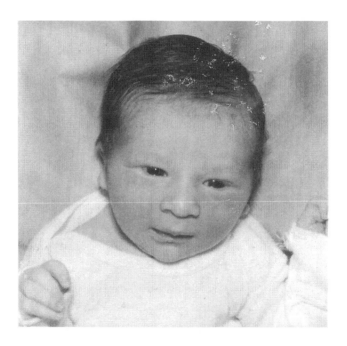

I remember taking Polaroids of Chase as soon as he was born as well as the nurse holding him up by his ankle to measure. I took the Polaroids out to Robin's mom and dad and they would shake them until they were developed each time, seeing the photos before me. They were so happy and proud and were both crying happy tears, just as I did, while our poor little Robin was just waking up from being put under so they could take Chase via C-Section.

I remember Chase being brought in and Robin holding so close, so tight, feeling so happy she had a beautiful healthy baby.

We filmed everyone around the bed talking and I remember Big Daddy just saying the time was 12:35 and Robin said, "WHAT? OMG—That's just a few minutes ago." I guess she felt she had been under for hours, but she had been taken into delivery room just after 12:00. I choked up and Big Daddy said "Poor Baby" and had happy tears too.

I was so proud of Chase. He was so beautiful and Robin was so proud of him too. I worked in PT at the Sports Rehab Clinic every day and each day when I got home, Robin was sitting on the couch holding Chase, looking at him, playing with him and would say each day, "Robbie, I think he is going to be a genius." I had never heard Robin sing before but after Chase was born, she sang to him everyday. The alphabet song was one of her favorites, so Chase could say the alphabet before he was a year old. I was so amazed with him being so active—he was sitting up, crawling and believe it or not, walking at only 6 months old. I bragged so much I had to bring him into the office, or rather had Robin bring him in, and stood him up on the floor and he walked right around the waiting room to the office, making me so proud, showing all my co-workers how good he was walking at only 6 months.

One evening I was lying on the couch with my son on my tummy, enjoying life with my wife making us something in the kitchen or maybe she was just watching me hold my son in peace and quiet as I had just got home from work all day at the Sports Rehab Clinic. Robin's mom and dad soon showed up at the door, coming in to see their grandson. I remember Big Daddy saying, "Well Rob, when are you going to start him boxing?" I said, "Never, I don't want Chase to ever box." Well, he laughed his ass off and said, "I hope he doesn't either, but I'm telling you right now he will have a whole lot more amateur fights than you ever did." I always loved and respected Big Daddy but I thought he was wrong this time for sure. I had 40 amateur fights and loved boxing as a professional.

Fast Forwarded 19 Years...

I just got off the phone with my wife Robin as I'm here on the Texas/Louisiana border, working in my first full-time job since 1999. Robin said Chase just called from the boxing camp in Milwaukee, saying he is leaving 11:30 pm Tuesday evening for Estonia to fight for the USA team in his first ever boxing match outside of the USA. Chase has 120 amateur bouts and is a 5X National Champion. I loved Big Daddy and often think of the things that he said would happen that did, years after he passed away the summer of 2000.

FIGHT #14
1996-01-15 Randy McGaugh, Beaumont Club, Kansas City, Missouri, USA W KO 5

With my father-in-law, I remember watching McGaugh fight in KC several times for years when I was still an amateur. Big Daddy always thought I could beat Randy and whomever he was fighting. Big Daddy was always ready to say to whomever was sitting close enough to hear, "Robbie could knock either one of them out tonight and he is an amateur still." He was always my biggest fan so when I did fight Randy, I knew I could not lose. I was always in good shape and always loved fighting, but I liked to drink some too. One night, my wife's brother came over wanting to talk for a while as he had some beer and was ready to tell me about some problems he was going through. That was fine, as I always loved Dave. He was one of my best friends with whom I spent many nights sitting around a campfire, on a fishing bank, or at his house out in the yard on the hammock, drinking a couple of beers.

Big Daddy and Robin Rae would always tell Dave or whoever else called if a fight was near, that "Robbie cannot do anything as he is training and has fight this weekend or next." I Love Robin so much for always supporting my boxing career and her dad who was a drinker himself when he was young, although, did not ever want me to drink. He would say, "Robbie, every time you drink you kill thousands of brain cells. You're a therapist now so quit drinking. Hell, you're in great shape, don't smoke, and I could strike a match on any part of your body, so why would you ruin all you've worked for drinking and smoking? That will do it, so don't ever do that crazy shit. Now hand me a cigarette, and let's get to Shotz Tavern so I can unwind, as you have driven me crazy worrying about you being prepared for this damn fight!" —I LOVED BIG DADDY!!!!!!!!

FIGHT #15
1996-04-24 Zennie Reynolds, Fireman's Local 77, Saint Joseph, Missouri, USA W KO 5 (8)

Three months later, I had another bout in St. Joseph at the Firemen's Hall against a kickboxer, Zennie Reynolds. He hit me late after the bell had rang to end the fourth round. I returned the favor so he kicked me and I began to fight fight fight, although bell had rang. I was throwing all I had as he pissed me off by kicking me. We had guys jumping into the ring to help the ref separate us and then after the start of the fifth round, it did not take me long to end the fight with a fifth round knockout.

I had Robin bring Chase to the fight so everyone could see our baby. After we got home, Robin wanted to hit me and told me she is never taking her baby to another fight again. As I've mentioned before, Robin doesn't like fighting and said she did not want her baby being around that violence anymore.

—I'm sitting here writing this in Shreveport, Louisiana after going home a couple of weeks ago to work with our son Chase, just a couple weeks after he turned 18, in his 100th amateur bout against a 30-year-old man.

CHASE WON BY 1ST ROUND KNOCKOUT!!!!
'KID DYNAMITE'

HAS ANYBODY TOLD YOU THEY LOVE YOU TODAY? I DO
ROBIN RAE CALLOWAY!

FIGHT #16
1996-06-03 Frank Minton, 28-28-2, Marriott Allis Plaza Hotel, Kansas City, Missouri, USA W KO 3 (8)

Won 1st Title WAA Canadian American Lt. Heavyweight Championship against former World Lt. Heavyweight Challenger from Indianapolis, IN

I remember this fight, as it was my first with my new promoter, Danny Campbell, who was both amateur and professional in the KC area. My father-in-law was never a fan of Danny's and would continue to point out everything wrong he did or did not do for the next few years.

I give Danny credit for keeping me busy in the ring, which allowed me to improve as I was continuing to stay in the gym and loved fighting and wanted to prove I was the best light heavyweight, cruiserweight, and eventually heavyweight around the Midwest.

I only remember Frankie Minton having many professional fights who was able to go nine rounds with my favorite fighter, Virgil Hill, who was Lt Heavyweight World Champion, so I really made myself train hard for the fight. I was aggressive and was able to knock Frankie out in just 3 rounds.

FIGHT #17
07-31-1996 Larry Fleming, Altoona, Iowa W KO 2

Danny told us next we had a bout in Iowa just few weeks later so we stayed in the gym and was again able to win by knockout. I loved knocking fighters out. I remember Fleming being a southpaw and at that time, the only lefthander I had faced was the guy I fought in the Olympic trials back in 1992 and I had lost. I controlled Fleming with my left jab as he was southpaw but shorter and I was able to control with keeping a busy left jab on him until he was ready to drop his right hand, followed by left hook which I was able to do in the 2nd round, winning by knockout. Afterwards, we stayed in the gym, continuing to improve with all my punches, including the jab, straight right hand, overhand right, left hook, and uppercut.

FIGHT #18
08-12-1996 Richard Wilson, Kansas City, Missouri W UD 6

The very next day Danny told me in only a couple of weeks I can get back in the ring in KC, but this time Danny was told they would allow me to fight Wilson in KC, but they had him in another fight a couple weeks later so I could not knock him out. My trainer, Steve Homan, agreed and was aware of this as well. The first round began and I was being aggressive and landed a right hand that dropped him right on his ass before the bell rang. After I got back to the corner, I remember Steve being mad and saying, "What in the hell you doing? I promised these guys you would carry him six rounds and if we piss these guys off you won't get any more fights." I said OK and went back out and jabbed his ass to death for the next five rounds. My brother-in-law was in the crowd, and he had brought down friends from his work who wanted to see me as well. I had to explain to my brother-in-law that night after we got home that I had to carry my opponent.

Well, he was upset, as he had told his friends I could really punch. Bruce wasn't as mad as my father-in-law Big Daddy was and he told me, "Never again, Robbie. You're the one in the ring and you're the one who can get cut from a punch, or head butt etc. so from now on, you win and win by knockout if you can—period." I loved Big Daddy for that and he told Danny, "Robbie will never carry anyone else, that is bullshit and I'm pissed you had him do that crazy shit anyway." Big Daddy was right again and I knew it, so I never did it again.

FIGHT #19
09-13-1996 Joe Harris, Des Moines, Iowa W KO 7
Live on ESPN *Friday Night Fights*

Top Rank had an ESPN bout in Iowa fairly close to home, and I was awarded my shot to be on TV again, My fights in Vegas had been on an Hispanic station, but this fight would be the first time on ESPN. I didn't know much about Harris besides him having a decent record, and after a few rounds I knew he could fight a little so I just continually tried to be the aggressor behind my left jab, letting the judges know I wanted to win and was willing to mix it up. I was able to stop Harris in the seventh round and get my first win on ESPN TV.

The big deal about this special night for me was not only getting a chance to fight on ESPN TV but also to have an opportunity to fight on the same card as Rocky Gannon, who people always say I looked a lot like. He was a great guy and my father-in-law and I always enjoyed watching his fights and seeing his toughness in the ring, win or lose.

I was a big fan of Butterbean Eric Esch just as many others were at that time, and he also fought on the. I remember Butterbean fighting to a draw with a good friend of mine at that time, Bill Eaton, who was a tough guy without a lot of amateur experience but was not scared to fight anyone and always came to fight. Bill and I were sparring partners early in my career and spent a lot of rounds in the ring together.

I returned from the fight to work the following week, enjoying the attention I received from getting a big win on ESPN. Soon thereafter, my boss Charlie wanted to send me to get some continuing education so I could be certified to do testing on several of the machines we had in our gym like the Cybex, or the Lumbar Extension machine. I would then be qualified to do testing for all employees hired by a local company to make sure they could pass with adequate Lower Back Strength before getting hired.

Charlie sent me to a continuing education course in San Francisco, California, which is where Robin and I had our honeymoon just five years before. We were very excited to return to the City of Love and loved being able to travel with our little Champ who was just nine months old. He was so active and was able to walk all around the airport and we loved having the champ go to the restaurants in San Francisco, eating all that sourdough bread, which may be the reason Chase loves bread to this day… hahaha

ROBIN AND I DIDN'T KNOW AT THIS TIME BUT LOOKING BACK AND PUTTING THE MATH TO IT, WE REALIZED THIS IS WHERE WE CREATED OUR SECOND BABY—RILEY RAE CALLOWAY—SHE WAS BORN NINE MONTHS LATER IN JUNE OF 1997.

I'm here writing my autobiography, realizing my wife was so happy with her baby boy and her husband having a great job in physical therapy and she was able to exercise regularly again, feeling better and getting herself into shape again. We decided to take Chase to Kentucky for a visit and we asked Robin's mom and dad to go with us, which they agreed to do. We decided to fly into Nashville and have my mom pick us up at the airport. I loved everyone seeing Chase who was not even nine months old but running all over the airport like a toddler with his long hair. Robin and I both loved his long black hair until my friends began to call him Billy Ray Cyrus, forcing me to cut the Lil Champ's hair. We had a great visit and I was very happy Robin's mom and dad got to see where I'm from and meet some family members, although they had already met my mother and were friends. I loved having them see how far I had come from the houses I had lived in as a kid to Robin and me now living on Robin Lane.

FIGHT #20
10-16-1996 Richard Green, Kansas City, Missouri
W KO 4

I was happy Danny was keeping his word, keeping me busy in the ring. I realized how lucky I was to have an employer like Charlie Edwards who always seem to be happy with working my schedule at the Sports Rehab Clinic around my boxing schedule. I know these early fights were important for me to gain experience in the ring with a fairly short amateur career, which is one of the reasons I understand how important amateur boxing is and how it just takes time being in the ring and understanding all the things that go on in a fight—the preparation, the training, the travelling to and from, and even and having everything worked out with your employer so you are able to make the fight happen.

I fought Green in the Westport area of Kansas City and although it was a rough area, everyone really seemed to enjoy the fights. It was a way for me to keep busy and continue to improve just by getting into the ring. Green was a more experienced fighter than me and had been in the ring with better opposition and was even taller than I was, making it the first time I had ever fought anyone taller. I was aggressive and landed some big shots that dropped him and although he got up, there was too much time left in the round for me not to finish with a good overhand right, knocking Green down and out.

FIGHT #21
11-27-1996 Steve Langley, Kansas City, Missouri
W KO 5

Langley was an experienced fighter with a good amateur background. I was told he was from Wichita, Kansas, the city of my first professional fight, so I was looking forward to the fight just a few days after my wife's birthday on November 22nd.

FIGHT #22
12-12-1996 Danny Thomas, St. Joseph, Missouri W PTS 12
Defense of WAA Canadian American Lt. Heavyweight Championship

Danny soon set up a 12-round defense of my American title I won from Minton on June third 1996. I was excited but a little nervous, as any fighter who has an opportunity to fight in a 12-rounder understands you just never know how you will react in the ring in the championship rounds until you have done it. I like Danny Thomas, as he was a real fighter who had fought many boxing greats and seemed to win or go the distance even if he lost. I got to know him better much later after our fight as he was a coach in Indiana of an amateur boxing team and I would see him often as I took our son Chase all over the country to events. We had a special bond only fighters understand. My friend, Danny Thomas.

FIGHT 23
04-02-1997 Ray Domenge, Lt. Heavyweight Champ, Kansas City, Missouri W KO 9
Won WAA Intercontinental Light Heavyweight Title

A few short months later, I found myself back in the ring and this would be in another 12-round bout at the Ameristar Casino in Kansas City against my toughest opponent to date—on paper anyway. Domenge was a good fighter from Nebraska with a lot of amateur experience. Many Kansas City Chiefs players came to see this bout at the new casino in Kansas City and my wife Robin sat ringside 7-months pregnant, leaving Chase with her mom for the night. Danny always did a good job promoting the bout to casinos and to local fans and he decided to make this bout for another title that I was happy to win. I know many of the belts I won do not mean a lot, but I always loved fighting for a title belt and with it being a 12-round bout, it prepared me for one day stepping into the ring with the world champ, knowing I did not have to worry about going the distance or preserving energy, as experience in the boxing ring is incomparable. I remember this bout for two things:

One, it was a good fight and I controlled with an aggressive jab, bringing the right hand regularly until I was able to catch Domenge, knocking him down and then out. He complained about me hitting him while he was on a knee, but I always hated when guys took a knee anyway. I know if you're hurt and don't want to get caught again, it can be smart thing to do, but I still hated it so maybe I did hit him little late. But I won easily by knockout in the ninth, beginning to separate myself from Midwest Lt Heavy's.

Two, my wife being 7-months pregnant with Riley Rae and sitting with many Chiefs players, including Tim Grunhard, and all the guys were smoking cigars. My wife Robin began to get a little sick and asked if he would put out his cigar. He said, "Yes, of course" then told all the guys, "Hey, this is Calloway's wife and she is pregnant so everyone put out your cigars." She was so happy and after telling me the story, I was so happy with My Man Big Tim Grunhard. I was always a fan of his as well as the other Chiefs! THANKS, CHAMPS!!!

FIGHT 24
06-03-1997 Tyrus Armstead, Kansas City, Missouri W KO 7 Defense of WAA Intercontinental Light Heavyweight Title

Well the next bout was scheduled for June third again at the Ameristar Casino in Kansas City and I asked Robin about it, as she was not due until the 24th of June. Of course, she would not go but would stay home, and I would go down with her dad and take care of business, make some money, and be home with 20 days before her due date. Robin began to get nervous, thinking of my fight while being at home and her blood pressure began to rise again just as it did with Chase when she went in for her doctor's appointment the day before the fight.

Big Daddy was told by Robin's mom that she had gone to the doctor for her check up and the doctor decided to schedule the C-Section for June 4th, the next day after my fight, as Robin's blood pressure had begun to rise again and Dr. Corder did not want to have to go through another emergency C-Section as we did with Chase. Robin told her mom and dad to keep it from me and not let me know until after the fight, as she did not want me to be worried about her and she would see me after the fight.

Tyrus really brought the fight and tried his best, punching with straight rights and left hooks, but I controlled with a left jab and was just too big and too strong of a Lt Heavyweight. I landed several big shots as well that led to several knockdowns in the fight, but he kept getting up until seventh round when I was able to put together some punches that would stop him for good with an impressive seventh round knockout. This knockout made us happy but we realized that I would not be able to make 175lb much longer. I was not the best at this time at staying away from alcohol, but I still always tried to make sure I was in great shape. I was never afraid to fight and never really got nervous. I felt the most comfortable after I would actually climb through the ropes to get into the ring. I know it may sound crazy to some, but throughout my entire career every time I climbed through the ropes I felt like I was home and I guess I felt all was in my hands now. That made me the most comfortable, I guess.

Well, everyone was able to keep the news of Robin's impending C-Section from me, and I just thought all was normal until the news reporter asked me how Robin was when he was doing my post-fight interview. Big Daddy almost hit the reporter when he said Robin had her check up that morning and her blood pressure was again rising too high and that Dr. Corder had scheduled the C-Section. I just said I was unaware and Big Daddy said, "We have not told you but we have time to drive home and you can be with Robin at the hospital." Well, we did and Robin had our beautiful baby girl the next morning around 8:30am. I was so proud and Riley looked like a Princess lying in her bed. I have never seen a baby so beautiful. Stole my heart from the first day I saw her. I love Chase and her the same but OMG, Riley Rae Calloway is the Prettiest Little Girl I have ever seen in my life!

MY ANGEL, RILEY RAE 'BUTTER' CALLOWAY, BORN JUNE 4th, 1997 at 10am.

FIGHT #25
08-08-1997 Eric Davis, Station Casino Kansas City, Missouri
W PTS 8 Live on ESPN *Friday Night Fights*

I scheduled the next fight at Ameristar Casino in Kansas City again. Danny promoted another ESPN bout and he was doing well keeping me busy. I was always in shape, ready to fight and with my new baby healthy and at home with our son Chase, I was feeling so blessed and really wanted to step up and make some money in the game for my family—Robin Rae, Chase Samuel, and Riley Rae Calloway. This bout would have me go the distance of 8 rounds but I was able to win unanimously on TV again. Happy!!!

FIGHT #26
10-09-1997 Daniel Salcedo, Altoona, Iowa W KO 3

The next bout would be against a guy who came in a little over the Lt Heavyweight limit of 175lbs but we made it happen anyway, and I would later become friends with Salcedo, but knocked him out in three rounds this night.

FIGHT #27
10-25-1997 Richard Wilson, St. Joseph, Missouri W KO 2

I continued to stay in the gym and got a call to fight Wilson, the guy I carried in Kansas City in front of my brother-in-law and his friends, but this time I agreed only if I could knock him out. I not only knocked him out, I knocked him into air about three feet.

Another big reason I wanted to not only win but win impressively was my mother and her younger brother, Ferlin, were coming to the fight. I was very close to Ferlin. He was the one who always loved fighting and is even the one who first put gloves on me as a young kid and would have me sparring several of his friends' younger brothers or cousins or anyone he could match me with as well as beating up on me at times. I have never forgotten it, Ferlin…

My mom's mother, my grandmother Mary Lorene Lindsey, came to the fight too. Well, actually they came to see me and Robin and our babies but got to go the fight as well.

I remember this fight not so much for the fight but the fact I got to have several of my family members carry out my belts I had won around the Midwest. But mainly I remember my grandmother giving Riley Rae 'Butter' her FIRST NICKNAME—'SMILEY RILEY.' She was always a happy smiling lil baby. My grandmother had eleven children of her own and many, many grandbabies, but she said that Riley Rae was the prettiest baby she had ever seen and Riley Rae is ALWAYS SMILING! SHE LOVED 'SMILEY RILEY.'

FIGHT #28
12-12-1997 Zennie Reynolds, Mason City, Iowa W KO 3

We got a call to return to Iowa and we had an opportunity to fight Zennie Reynolds, Kickboxing Champion of St. Louis, Missouri. Although we had beat him before, he was a well-conditioned man who in our last fight kicked me, leading to a brawl in the ring which I went on to win by knockout. It had been an exciting time early in my career. I picked up where I left off from our first fight and did not want to let Zennie get any confidence built up, so I pressured from the beginning and was able to knock him out in three rounds.

FIGHT #29
02-10-1998 Mike Pearman Lt. Heavyweight Champ, St. Joseph, Missouri W KO 3
Won World WAA Light Heavyweight Title

This next bout was called a world title and my promoter put on the bout in my hometown of St. Joseph, Missouri, but I considered it just a Midwest fight. I was happy to show I did deserve to step up and was ready after I KO'd Pearman easily in three rounds.

It was now 1998 and Big Daddy and I were constantly watching the fights on TV, either on ESPN or *Tuesday Night Fights*. I was still making the Lt Heavyweight Limit of 175 pounds, working hard every-day. Soon we saw Rocky Gannon on TV and he won a title bout and soon thereafter lost to Dominick 'Hurricane' Carter. Big Daddy, Danny, and others began to try to put me in the mix, thinking I would have a good chance at winning and soon get a chance at a world championship.

That year, St. Joseph, Missouri won the All American City award. Danny had set up a time for me to go back to my hometown in Kentucky to talk to some people about me having an opportunity to defend my belt that I had recently won. He was just never able to get the interest raised around my hometown or where I went to high school. Because of our moving so much and me going to so many different schools and living in several different towns and states, I consider my hometown as St. Joseph, Missouri, which is where I have lived since I was a teenager. However, I still feel a part of Ohio County, Kentucky, which is where I spent the majority of my school years, including all of my 4 years in high school. But I also will never forget the years I spent in Georgetown, Kentucky and as I have mentioned, Facebook has been great to reconnect with so many old friends.

After me winning a USA title, Danny set up a time for me to also speak at my high school in the gym and although it was a short time and a small presentation, I'm glad I was able to prove it was only the beginning of my long successful career and it was with all the television fights, winning five of six on ESPN over the years and with the technical draw on Showtime as well as a couple of wins on local PPV as well as the two local guys we were able to show on TV for months from our local cablevision.

FIGHT #30
05-19-1998 Tyler Hughes, St. Joseph, Missouri W KO 8 Defense of World WAA Light Heavyweight Title

This fight was the last time I made the weight of 175lbs. I trained hard and was tired of waiting to get a big fight, but I made sure I was continuing to win, which is the most important. I was 28-2 with 21 wins by Knockout.

FIGHT #31
07-10-1998 Lonnie Knowles, Station Casino Kansas City, Missouri
W KO 3 Defense of World WAA Light Heavyweight Title
(Last Light Heavyweight Bout)

This bout was to defend the title I had won and defended a couple times, but I could not make weight anymore at 175 pounds. The good thing was my opponent came in heavy as well so we did not have to pay a fine or anything. The title was just vacated, as I never fought Light Heavyweight again. Looking back now, it's hard to believe I was ever 175 pounds.

My son Chase Fights at 175 pounds and is 18 years old. I had my last fight in the Lt Heavyweight Division in 1998, then to cruiserweight at 190lbs.

FIGHT #32
9-30-1998 Jason Nicholson, Ultimate Fighting Champ of Oklahoma City, OK, Station Casino Kansas City, Missouri W PTS 6

This next bout was against a guy who has been my friend as well as a friend to my wife and son for many years now. At the time, the Midwest promoters began to put on fights that would go on the record as a win for the winner but be called a No-Contest on the losers record. Therefore, it was basically a sparring match, only in front of crowd with no headgear, no shirt, and little fight gloves. I considered it a fight. I said, "No I don't wanna be no part of that" and the Promoter said, "His manager cannot have him knocked out as he has him fighting in another town next week." I said, "I don't even know if I can knock him out." I won every round just boxing and was awarded the decision.

FIGHT #33
10-10-1998 Dominic Carter Former Lt. Heavyweight World
Champ, St. Joseph, Missouri W KO 2
Bout was Refereed by legendary "Let's get it on" Mills Lane

Jason Redmond, Mills Lane, and Rob

I felt my first big fight came in 1998 when I fought Dominick 'Hurricane' Carter from New Orleans. The fight was refereed by Miles Lane, who had just a few months before refereed Mike Tyson's bout where Tyson bit off a piece of Evander Holyfield's ear.

Big Daddy and I had watched the champ Dom on a regular basis. We were able to bring him into St. Joseph, Missouri for the biggest

93

bout in that town ever. I trained hard every day, sparring regularly as well as putting in the running and all the work that comes with being a champion. I knew this was my biggest fight and I took it very seriously. I wanted to win and win impressively. Everything in my life was going well with Robin, Chase almost 3 years old, and Riley Rae a year and a half. We received the contract for the fight. They required Dom and me to come in at 185 pounds instead of the usual cruiserweight limit of 190. I agreed and came in at 183½ for the bout. Big Daddy was very happy and Dom came in at 184, outweighing me. It was the biggest crowd up until that time at the Civic Arena for boxing, or perhaps for any event, and the fans all came out to see if the guy they had been hearing about was going to have a chance of being a boxing champion or was just being blown up by the media and this promoter from Kansas City.

After we both entered the ring, the animosity of the crowd could be felt. Soon after the introductions were made, it was Referee Miles Lane's turn. He said, "Men, you already had the instructions in the locker room. I expect a tough clean fight. This is what the people came to see. Any Questions from the Blue Corner? Any Questions from the Red Corner?... LET'S. GET. IT. ON!!!"

My Father-in-law was my Head Cornerman and I loved the way he stepped up and handled business just like I knew he would. He was very proud as he and I had watched Dominic Carter on the television in his basement hundreds of times on tape, as Big Daddy always recorded the fights.

I'm excited all over again as I sit here writing this story, thinking about it being the first time I had ever been knocked off my feet and by the guy Big Daddy and I had watched on tape in his basement so many times before. Well, I got up and looked at Miles Lane and said, "Yes Sir, I'm fine." He said, "Ok, box." Soon Dom began to see I was not injured as he did land a good shot that knocked me down but I was 100% recovered by end of the count. I began to exchange with the Champ, landing several big shots myself as he continued to try to get me with another big punch. I caught Dom on the way in and although knocked backwards, he was punching at the same time. Judge Miles Lane did not see how badly the punch hurt Dom and did not give him a count, so I got right back on him and backed him into his corner. I threw a right hand that came up short but followed with what I still call the Best Left Hook of my 92-Professional-Fight Career.

The punch knocked out Dominic 'Hurricane' Carter at the end of the 2nd round, leaving me the Champ to the City of St. Joseph, Missouri from that moment on.

I HAVE DEEMED THIS MY FIRST 'BIG' FIGHT.

I've mentioned Facebook throughout my autobiography and another one of the great things I have found is the ability to touch base with so many fighters, many my opponents. It is so nice to speak to so many great fighters such as Dom and let them know I was a fan of theirs before we fought and I will always be a fan, as I realize how great they are and how much I respect real fighters. I have for years shared my stories with my son and have taken him across the USA, as he fought as an amateur. Chase always knows them by first name and I'm very fortunate and feel very blessed that Dom and his trainer invited me to dinner after I let them know I was coming to Orange, Texas to take my full time job in physical therapy. I loved letting my wife and kids know about the great visit I had with Dom and his trainer who took me out to eat. He is a real Champ!

FIGHT #34
01-16-1999 John Moore, Golden Eagle Casino Horton, Kansas
W KO 5

I felt I was getting close to getting a world title fight after my win over Dom, so we decided to stay busy. I was scheduled for a fight in Kansas at the beginning of 1999 and I was able to knock out John Moore, looking forward to a big year.

I had been cut on a couple of occasions in the amateurs and even on a couple of occasions already in the Pro's. John and I bumped heads, leaving a small cut on my right eyebrow that required a few stitches. Big Daddy was able to take care of it between rounds and I was able to continue my busy strong pace that led me to win by Knockout in the fifth round.

FIGHT #35
02-19-1999 Shawn Clarkson, Burlington, Iowa, Pretty straight
Right Hand W KO 1

I healed up quickly from the cut over my right eye and just a month later, I had an opportunity to fight in Iowa at a casino. I was able to land one of my best right hands that dropped my opponent face first, leading to another win by knockout. I've had several one-punch Knockouts over the years, but I still rate this one as one of my best and favorite. I loved knocking men out and especially loved when they fell face first, not even able to raise their own hands or arms up to cushion the blow. Is this wrong? I LOVED IT, DAMN IT I LOVED IT. OKAY, JUST A LIL PROBLEM MAYBE...

I've posted this story on Facebook before but I wanted to share in book as I still remember when I'm alone in Texas...

Robin Rae and I would like to cruise around the town and drive boulevard with the kids when they were young. Riley Rae would always get a good nap. But this time I had just beat Dominick 'Hurricane' Carter and was preparing for the Spinks fight. Billboards were up and I was on TV and in the paper often. We were cruising through town, and Chase said, "Dad, are you Rob Calloway?" I start to wipe the tears from my eyes and Robin said, "What did you say, Chase?" He said, "Is Dad Rob Calloway?" (I have tears in my eyes now just writing this.) Robin Rae said, "Yes Chase, of course" and he said, "I'm going to be a champion like Daddy one day." Well, Chase has been 'my champ' since the day he was born, but I really never realized, at this time anyway, that he would one day grow up to be 'Kid Dynamite.'

We had already been discussing a fight between Daryl Spinks, the son of Leon Spinks from St. Louis, and myself, and we knew it would be a big fight in St. Joseph.

FIGHT #36
04-03-1999 Darrell Spinks, son of Heavyweight Champion Leon Spinks and Nephew of World Heavyweight Champion Michael Spinks, St. Joseph, Missouri W PTS 12
Won IBA Continental Americas Cruiserweight Title

I really felt comfortable coming down from around 195 to make the weight limit of 190 at cruiserweight. I was always in shape, staying in the ring so much and in the gym, never taking more than a week off after each fight. After a lot of negotiations, the fight was made for Calloway vs. Spinks and just putting the billboards up around town, the citizens began to talk about it and tickets were selling quick. Daryl's brother Cory, also the son of the legendary Leon Spinks and both also the nephews of Michael Spinks, was also on the card, but the of Calloway–Spinks fight was the one everyone seemed to be talking about. Cory fought one of the first bouts and looked great with a win by knockout. That had the crowd ready for the main event and Daryl and I did not disappoint, as we put on a fight going twelve rounds and people got to see that their hometown boy had potential to not only get a world title fight but also to win a title.

I have said how much I love meeting all the fighters and now years later, having an opportunity to see them. Several years after this fight, much later towards the end of my career, I had an opportunity to see Daryl again, as I had signed a promotional deal with the guys from St. Louis. They had invited me down to watch Corey Spinks fight and afterwards I was being introduced to fighters around ring and other people invited to fight by the promoter and I noticed Corey coming with several close friends and family. One was Daryl who I yelled at, saying hello and he came right up to me and gave me a big hug. I was so happy to introduce him to my son who I took along with me to watch the fight in St. Louis and he shook Chase's hand. I really appreciated Daryl doing so and I was happy my son got to meet him, as he had heard so much about him since he was young kid. Chase did not go to the fight between Daryl and me since he was only 4 years old at the time.

I've been told the fight is still talked about to this day, as my friend said he just heard it at the barbershop last weekend or at parties of friends. Anyway, not much can make an old fighter feel better.

Rob, Michael Spinks, and Chase

THANKS FOR REMEMBERING!

Around this time, an auction for some charity was held in St. Joseph. I'm not sure what it was for, but I remember it was a great event and I wanted to take my wife to it after receiving the invitation. So I bought a table and invited some of our best friends to come along. They were going to auction off a Dinner at the Thedinger house, which was one of Robin's favorite homes on Ashland Avenue in our hometown of St. Joseph. I placed a bid after there were several others and soon the bid was $500. I stuck up my card and then went to $700, then $800, then $1000. I kept putting my card up as I had a pocketful of money, coming off the win against Spinks and I was feeling like a damn Champ. But I guess I forgot I was bidding against a man who had a bank full of money. . Anyway, I asked the man, Al Purcell, to let me have the dinner so after we got to over $1500 dollars, I was the winner. I have became friends with him and his lovely wife and I thank him for letting me give some of my best friends a great night on the town that we will never forget.

Mr. Thedinger opened a bottle of Vodka that was special from Russia, I believe, and poured us a glass, saying, "Rob, it's a sipping wine." "Thank you, sir" as yes, it was! HOT… Great Stuff.

I loved having my great friends John Gillaspie and his wife Dotty, Steve Shanks and his wife Seanna, David Lee Reynolds and his wife Denise, Dirk Colbach and his wife Julie with us that night.

What a lovely couple the Thedinger's were, just absolutely perfect to us, sharing their home and being such great entertainers!!!! Special night… Time moves on in all of our lives and we have lost some of the great friends since then, but I loved them all and I'm so glad I got to have them to share this special night with me and my lovely wife Robin Rae. Thank you, Friends!

FIGHT #37
05-23-1999 Nathaniel Miles, Harrah's Hotel and Casino Kansas City, Missouri W PTS 8 Live on Fox Sports Television Network

My next bout was against Nate Miles at Harrah's Casino in KC and also on Fox Sports. Honestly I thought I knocked him out but I guess I won an 8-round decision. I remember landing some big blows on highlights from TV, but he was tough man who took me to the 8th round decision.

FIGHT #38
07-10-1999 Dan Kosmicki, Civic Arena St. Joseph, Missouri
W KO 6

I knew we were getting close to a title fight so I wanted to stay busy. With not a lot of quality sparring around the area at the time, I instead fought a guy from Nebraska who was tough guy and would fight anybody. Danny set up a bout between him and me again at the Civic Arena in St. Joseph. Kosmicki always brought his best but was too slow and I won by KO in the 6th.

FIGHT #39
09-01-1999 Donnie Penelton, St. Joseph, Missouri W PTS 8

I was anticipating a world title fight so until then, we accepted an outdoor fight at our local casino against Pendleton, a journeyman who went the distance with everybody. I threw a lot of hard punches, trying to knock him out, but he kept coming until the end of the fight with me winning a unanimous decision.

FIGHT #40
11-12-1999 Kenny Keene 3X World Champ, Boise, Idaho
L PTS 12 for IBA World Cruiserweight Championship–190 lbs.

Keene had fought a rematch on TV with Carter, who took him the distance, prior to my KO victory over Carter, which was the reason we had to keep busy fighting other guys. When the fight was finally made against Keene, Danny set up a camp in Las Vegas where I was able to get good sparring and additional training from Kenny Adams, who was a great trainer of the USA team as well as was in the corner years later of Ruslan Chagaev, who eventually became World Heavyweight Champion and whom I fought on Showtime. Adams noticed I had some power and could box with sound fundamentals but knew Keene always came to fight as well. He asked my trainer, Steve, "How much running is Rob doing?" Steve told him of the 7 mile runs around the track at the University of Las Vegas as well as all the training before sparring. Adams told Steve, "You don't have to push so much with

Calloway as he is not cheating on you. He is a hard worker and putting in all the time as well as all the sparring." I remember Adams also saying, "It's not my business, but I would say cut back on the training a little if his weight is fine, especially all the unnecessary running." Steve felt he knew better and continued with pretty much the same routine. I'm not saying it would have been any different, but I felt a respected trainer was saying the same things I was feeling as well. I also felt I should have stayed closer during the fight, putting punches together but in reality, now I understand at that time I probably would not have been able to fight like I would have nowadays. I feel I learned so much more with the correct way of fighting with different styles later in my career with Marshall Kauffman and feel not only would I have beat Kenny for the world championship, but I would have beaten other cruiserweight champions from that time if I'd had Marshall Kauffman in my Corner.

FIGHT #41
02-18-2000 Dan Kosmicki Lincoln, NE Burlington, Iowa
My 1st Heavyweight Fight W KO 2

A few months later, we were able to regroup. I did not take Steve Homan as my trainer any longer, just feeling that I was ready to move on and even continue to move up to fight bigger men. Kosmicki was my first heavyweight fight in Burlington Iowa after we watched the local heavyweight who was the main event on the card that night, who was coming off a big win and a great showing overseas in Denmark versus a fighter who would soon fight Mike Tyson in his return to the ring.

What we did not know was after the main event was fought, he grabbed the microphone and said he wanted to fight Rob Calloway next to show everyone who was the best heavyweight in the Midwest.

103

I had just won my first heavyweight fight, but I was pissed anyway for him assuming he could beat me.

"2000" WAS MY FIRST FIGHT IN THE HEAVYWEIGHT DIVISION. I FOUGHT HEAVYWEIGHT THE REMAINDER OF MY CAREER UNTIL MAKING A RETURN FOR A FEW FIGHTS AT CRUISERWEIGHT TO MAKE SOME MONEY, THEN RETURNED TO HEAVY FOR LAST COUPLE OF FIGHTS AT 41 AND 42. ALL AMERICAN PRIZEFIGHTER...

FIGHT #42
03-31-2000 Troy Weida, IBA Super Cruiserweight Champ, Burlington, Iowa W KO 1 Won IBA Super Cruiserweight Title Bout Viewed on Tape-delayed Pay Per View Television

A fight between Troy Weida and me was made and the TV personalities who were there to cover me in my first heavyweight fight had some big news to report to our city in St. Joseph.

My wife Robin Rae put together a fan bus for all who wanted to go to the fight, which sold out pretty soon. I went up early, of course, but rode the fan bus back with Robin and what a great trip it was.

Before the fight, I was pissed at Weida for calling me out and I felt like the promoter and his people already knew it was coming without letting me know anything. When I got my time on the microphone during our first press conference, I said I was looking forward to kicking his ass and was not promising a knockout but was guaranteeing a win, which fired everyone up seeing me really mad for the first time on camera and in the heavyweight division where I was weighing only around 205 but in great shape, and I always felt I had a good punch with either hand.

The fight blew up around his town as well as in St. Joseph as soon as the news got back that we were fighting for the IBA Heavyweight

Title. He was coming off a great showing in Denmark and I guess many still did not feel I was the fighter the media was making me out to be. I was very fired up all through camp and went into the fight mad. I was pissed in the interviews leading up to the fight as well as the last interview prior to the fight by the PPV camera guys where I again predicted I would WIN. I did not say by knockout as he had just fought big good heavyweight in Denmark and was able to go the distance with a big puncher, but I really thought I was going to win and was READY… READY… READY…

IT WAS AN EASY KNOCKOUT IN ONE ROUND. MY WIFE WAS SO HAPPY and LOOKED BEAUTIFUL AS ALWAYS ON FIGHT NIGHT!!!

FIGHT #43
07-28-2000 Lorenzo Boyd, former Iron Mike opponent, St. Joseph, Missouri W KO 6

Boyd was guy who was a sparring partner for most fighters and had a KO loss to Iron Mike Tyson early in his career which was one of his claims to fame, but I easily outboxed and knocked out Lorenzo Boyd's smart ass out cold in the sixth round after beating him up like I told him I was gonna do first. It's ok, yes he pissed me off and yes THIS WHITE 'BOY' DID KNOCK HIM OUT LIKE I SAID I WOULD DO AND HE DESERVED IT. Believe that. Peace.

I REMEMBER BIG DADDY SAYING IN THE LOCKER ROOM BEFORE FIGHT, "ROB I'M PROUD OF THE WAY YOU HAVE WORKED TO MAKE YOUR BODY INTO A TRUE HEAVYWEIGHT. I NEVER THOUGHT YOU WOULD OUTGROW THE 190 POUND CRUISERWEIGHT DIVISION, BUT YOU HAVE." I SAID, "THANKS AND I LOVE YA, BIG DADDY." HE SAID, "I LOVE YOU TOO."

A COUPLE OF MONTHS LATER, JERRY 'BIG DADDY' REDMOND WAS MOWING HIS GRASS AND HAD A HEART ATTACK. I LOVED HIM AND STILL MISS HIM OFTEN. I KNOW HE LOVED HIS DAUGHTER ROBIN RAE VERY MUCH AND I KNOW HE WAS HAPPY WE FOUND EACH OTHER AND HE WAS ALWAYS VERY PROUD OF OUR BABIES, CHASE AND RILEY RAE!

FIGHT #44
11-11-2000 Jason Nicholson Ultimate Fighting Champ Oklahoma City, OK St. Joseph, Missouri W KO 3

Nicholson stepped in to fill in for an opponent who backed out at the last minute so I outboxed Jason until the Ref stepped in to stop the bout.

FIGHT #45
04-13-2001 James (Quick) Tillis, St. Joseph, Missouri W KO 9
Tillis was a Heavyweight Champ of the World challenger, who lost a 10-round decision to Iron Mike Tyson

Our next bout was another one Danny Campbell promoted in St. Joseph, Missouri against James 'Quick' Tillis. Fight fans remember Tillis as he was the first man to go the distance with Iron Mike Tyson back in the day when Iron Mike was knocking out everyone with awesome destruction. Quick not only went the distance but put on a good show, winning several rounds. This was one of the bouts on HBO since Mike had signed the big promotional campaign. Quick had actu-

106

ally gone 15 rounds versus Mike Weaver for the Heavyweight Championships, which was one of the last 15-round title fights in history. I knew all this and really respected Quick. I had watched the fight years ago in the 80's and always looked up to Quick as a real fighter who deserved respect from other fighters like myself trying to make a name in this tough business we have chosen. I remember the slur in his speech and the swagger as he spoke about the wars with real fighters back in the day like Earnie Shavers who many, including the Greatest of All Time, would name as one of the hardest punchers in boxing. I trained hard as I could, running each morning down that street we lived close to. So many cars would honk and wave each morning and I'm not sure they ever realized they were one of so many that would wave making me feel good, keeping in my mind how much I wanted to win. Danny brought in Referee Joe Cortez, a legendary referee in boxing from Las Vegas, to referee the fight. Joe did a great job and looking back, I actually thought of Quick as being old at that time. I remember thinking if I'm going to amount to anything in this fight game I love, I better not lose. Before the fight, I would go to sleep and think how I could beat James Quick Tillis. Hell, I love and respect him for his fights with real World Champions, including the Baddest Man on the Planet at the time, Iron Mike Tyson. Quick went 10 rounds with him and won several important fights, even Evander 'The Real Deal' Holyfield and Earnie Shavers. What the hell am I doing? I drove myself crazy, wanting to run, lift weights, hit the heavy bags, speed bag, double end bag, uppercut bag, spar, shadow box and probably did in my sleep.

The fight was a good fight and Quick knew it would be his last chance as well, so he got into the best shape possible. He brought his good footwork and hard quick left jab that I was impressed with even as I tried to be first or counter with mine. I soon began to put my punches together and land the right hand following with the left hook until Quick was in the corner and began to take too many punches. The great Ref did what he was brought in for and that was to prevent Quick from taking too many unnecessary blows to the head. I won a great fight, although I was unable to lean on it too much due the age of Quick, and I realized I had only beaten a faded version of a once great fighter. I went into Quick's locker room after the fight while he was sitting on the bench with his trainer and close friend, Ronnie Warrior. Ronnie was sitting close with his arm around the Champ. I went in and sat on the other side of Quick and put my arm around his other shoulder. Quick looked at me, so I said, "Quick I want to say I LOVE YOU MAN AND WAS ALWAYS A FAN AND I WANT TO SAY I KNOW I ONLY BEAT A VERSION OF YOURSELF." QUICK TILLIS HUGGED ME AND SAID, "DON'T SAY THAT AGAIN AS I TRAINED HARD AND CAME TO FIGHT AND YOU WON AND I BELIEVE YOU WILL GO ON TO DO GREAT THINGS IN THIS SPORT. I LOVE YOU TOO LIL BROTHER!"

THIS WAS ANOTHER ONE OF MY HAPPIEST MOMENTS IN BOXING. NOT THE FACT THAT I WON BUT THE FACT I EARNED RESPECT AND LOVE FROM A GREAT FIGHTER WHO I LOOKED UP TO. FEW YEARS LATER, I DID A FIGHT TO RAISE MONEY FOR A FALLEN CHAMP THAT I ALSO HAD GREAT ADMIRATION FOR, GREG PAGE, SO I CALLED QUICK AND HIS TRAINER RONNIE WARRIOR TO COME IN FOR THE FIGHT AND SIT RINGSIDE AND BE GUEST OF HONORS, WHICH THEY DID. I BELIEVE GREG EVEN BEAT QUICK BACK IN THE DAY WHEN HE WAS 'QUICK' TILLIS.

I RETIRED QUICK FOR GOOD AS HE NEVER FOUGHT AGAIN AND I WOULD FIND OUT AFTER LOOKING BACK PREPARING FOR MY BOOK THAT MY LAST FIGHT - MY 92nd WAS IN AUSTRALIA AND I TOO WAS 42 CLOSE TO 43 YEARS OLD IN MY LAST FIGHT BEFORE I WOULD RETIRE FOR GOOD.

It is a great part of my life to become friends with Hasim 'Rock' Rahman. It is good to know we value so many of the same things, even though we believe in different gods. Or maybe the same. We know soon enough. But I have always had respect for the hardest puncher I ever fought in my career and always had a lot of love for his sons who are great young men and have been to our house with Sharif and sparred with my son Chase many times.

This Lil Guy didn't have a chance! I remember when I came in to pick up all the amateur boxers to take to weigh-in for the Ringside World Tournament one year, Robin pointed at Chase as he was 8 years old and had his little boxing bag and just assumed he was going to go along to the weigh-in and fight as you can begin at 8 years old as its 8 and 9 year olds that make up the first bracket in the tournament. I told Chase, "You train for one year and if you still want to, I promise I will take you there next year." Well Chase just loved the sport from day one. The next year Chase had his first ever boxing match in late November, a few days after turning 9 year old. He won all three rounds against an older kid and looked so damn good, his poor mommy just couldn't believe it. As she was crying, she said, "OMG, you guys are going to kill me as Chase is so good he is never going to quit this damn sport after you have already driven me CRAZY!" TRUE, ROBIN RAE WAS AT MY FIRST AMATEUR FIGHT AT 19 YEARS OLD AND MY FIRST PROFESSIONAL FIGHT AT 22 YEARS OLD AS WELL AS MY LAST AT 42 YEARS OLD.

OUR BABY GIRL RILEY RAE 'BUTTER' CALLOWAY

Riley Rae grew up in a boxing world as well and she has always loved being a dancer, cheerleader, and even volleyball and basketball player, but she has always loved dancing the best. She recently was offered a scholarship in Kansas for both dancing and track. I'm SO proud of her for all she has done and become. I never allowed her to box. I fought, as I am what I am, but I couldn't let my Beautiful Baby take a punch!!!!! Robin said, "What about my Beautiful Baby?" meaning Chase. I said, "He wants to and he is a boy." ROBIN THEN PUNCHED ME… ouch!!!!!

We Loved Team Calloway Family Health and Fitness and Team Calloway Boxing. I have decided after all the years and fights and memories, I am very happy we owned and operated 'Team Calloway' for eleven years. Robin and I would not change a thing. I feel 100% that it was a great atmosphere for our children to be raised in as they are both very health conscious and active and I really believe kids need to see their parents active and wanting to live a healthy lifestyle to be motivated themselves.

Robin and I decided we would attempt to do what I had been telling her we should do for the past year and that was to open our own health club and boxing gym where I could train here at home and bring in sparring partners when needed and we could raise our kids in a perfect atmosphere like a family health and fitness club. So it began and after I went into the bank and asked for money, they said, "rob, you have to get it drawn up on a business plan to show how it will work out so we can sell it to bank members who sit on the board." so I went home and drew it all up what I felt I needed including the building robin and I had picked out, which was close to our home and we felt this would really work. We opened team Calloway family health and fitness club in may 2001. I had few wonderful friends who helped me come up with money I needed, including dr. Doug stokes, David Reynolds, Dick Rochambeau and Dick DeShon. They were friends and supporters of my entire boxing career. David Reynolds was the man who saw me running at the YMCA, training for the Kansas City Golden Gloves, and Dick Rochambeau had a business next to my father-in-law's and would see me training daily as well. I worked next door to Dr. Doug Stokes' orthopedic practice and he and his wife became friends and fans and would come to see me box at several shows over the years as well. The other was Dick DeShon, who was a local business man and he and his wife went to the same church as robin and me and one day Mignon, Dick's wife said hello to me outside of the church and said she watched my interview on television and was impressed and loved the way I talked about love for my wife Robin and our children. A few minutes later, Dick said, "Hey, introduce me. I want to meet the Champ too." Well, they were great friends and Robin and I truly loved all of the backers of Team Calloway, including Bob Norton who also supported us with an equal amount as other investors, however we paid his back a year later as asked. I'm glad he and his wife got to enjoy the health club for the first year free of charge for helping us out with start-up money. I really appreciate each and every person who helped me in any way from the time I came to Missouri at

17 years old until I left for Texas at 45 years old. It was a dream come true to share my boxing life with everyone but most importantly to be able to raise our kids in the healthy atmosphere of a health club, seeing everyone exercise and do boxing classes. It was just a great life I really enjoyed for 10 years. The greatest to me was being able to share so much time with my wife Robin who was there day and night when I was off fighting around the world. I'm not sure she will say she loved it as much as me, but I bet she would. Robin Rae was in great shape and looked beautiful and so did our children. It was a great part of our life from 2000 to 2011. We moved from our first location on woodbine to St. Joseph Avenue from 2011-2012, which was right down the street from Lafayette High School where our kids both went. We were there only one year before I returned to physical therapy as a traveler for a couple of years then taking my first full time job here on the Gulf coast in Orange, Texas.

I think one of the most fun and valuable things I did at Team Calloway was to create 'Team Calloway Box Aerobics.' I would get only 4 people, one in each corner, and I would hold the punch mitts. The class would begin when the bell rang with class working for 8 rounds and punching the mitts with 4, 6, or 8 punches with either a straight punch, hook, uppercut, or overhead, each being called out prior to beginning each punching session and each class member got to punch around the ring. Then when the 30-second bell rang, whoever was on me, making sure each person got 2 30-second times, the person would punch non-stop for 30 seconds as hard as possible. It was so much fun and such a great class. I should have promoted it much more and I believe it could be so much bigger, but our son Chase has gotten to continue with it now as his class, and I'm glad as he cannot schedule enough classes. It's fun and the best way to exercise, getting strength, cardio, balance, and stamina all in one 45-minute class and then doing some abdominal work together afterwards. FUN FUN FUN! CALL CHASE 'KID DYNAMITE' CALLOWAY.

FIGHT #46
08-18-2001 Craig Brinson, Dallas, Texas W KO 6

Somehow Danny Campbell arranged for Dave Gorman from Ft Worth Texas to come in and watch the fight between Quick and me. The next morning, Dave took me to breakfast and said he and his wife Loretta managed five fighters who would go on to become World Champions and believed I could be their sixth. They arranged for my next bout to be in Dallas, Texas where I would fight a journeyman, Craig Brinson. I won that fight by a sixth-round Knockout.

FIGHT #47
09-21-2001 Tue Bjorn Thomsen 1996 Silver Medalist, Vejle, Denmark L PTS 12 IBC Super Cruiserweight Title 3

Dave and Loretta were both nice people with good hearts and loved the sport of boxing. I still remember Dave taking me to Denmark to fight Tue Bjorn Thomsen for the World Cruiserweight Title. I loved Dave but he loved his alcohol and did not ever know when to say enough was enough. He drank on the plane all the way over to Frankfurt, Germany from Dallas, Texas until the stewardesses were forced to cut him off.

Dave was my head trainer at this time with my brother-in-law Jason Redmond being the second in charge in my corner. I did have a good camp and was able to get a lot of quality sparring in Ft. Worth and even drove a few miles over to Dallas to get some more. I remember several things about this great bout. This was my second shot at a world title after losing a 12-round decision to Keene in Boise, Idaho in 1999, not quite 2 years earlier, and also this fight was a few days after 9/11 and the world was confused with everything that was happening. I just remember how much I hated being away from my family although there was nothing I could do; it was just as scary being home as it was being away from Robin, Chase, and Riley Rae when all the terror was going on.

I was in training camp in Ft. Worth ten days before the fight. After running along the river one morning for my roadwork, I came back to the hotel I was staying at and turned on the TV to see the Twin Towers. Actually, one of them had just been hit by a plane and soon while I was watching, the other was blasted into by another plane. So sad and scary and then I called my wife and stayed on the phone with her for the next hour, not knowing what was happening and just scared with me being so far away in Ft. Worth and getting ready to fly out of the country for the first time to fight for a world championship. I remember all the scary craziness that had the whole world frightened. I also remember being one of the first flights to be able to leave the country, as security was so high.

We flew to Frankfurt, Germany and then on to Vejle, Denmark for the title fight. They had set up a training facility so we could finish up camp there and I remember everyone was nice and respectful regarding the hateful plane attacks from the terrorists. I remember I had a good ovation when they announced the red corner, "'ALL AMERICAN PRIZEFIGHTER' ROB CALLOWAY..."

A million viewers tuned in on the Danish television network.

One of the other things I remember was seeing Virgil 'Quicksilver' Hill being in Tue's corner and with him at all the meetings. I said, "Virgil, I have always looked up to you and respected you and my first time fighting out of the USA and you're in my opponent's corner." He said, "Rob, they brought me over to spar with Tue to prepare him for you and they are also getting me a fight." Well, I always respected the champ, Virgil 'Quicksilver' Hill. I will always remember him being a great man and real champ who gave me so many props after our fight in Denmark, not only that night and the next day but years later when I saw him at an amateur event with my son. When he saw me across the ring, he walked right around and said, "Rob." I said, "Who are you?" He said, "I'm Virgil Hill" and I felt like shit not recognizing him right

114

away as I had told him he was one of my favorite of all time and my father-in-law and I watched every one of his fights we could for as long as I could remember. I guess we all get a little older and look different in our street clothes, even Virgil. He made me so proud, telling my son, "Your dad won that fight in Denmark and it should have been by TKO as Tue came back to the corner every round after the eighth, saying, "Stop it; I can't go on." Virgil said he would talk him into getting up and then push him back out there. I said, "Thanks a lot, Champ." Tue was a Tuff guy and I respected him for the fight.

RIP CHAMP TUE BJORN THOMSEN.

FIGHT #48
04-26-2002 Marcus Rhode, Civic Arena, St. Joseph, Missouri
W KO 3

The next bout was against a longtime friend who was a Missouri Western Football player and even fought as an amateur for me for a little while, winning a few titles. This game we all love is a business as well and I knew he could use the money at the time, so I called Craig Cummings to set the bout up. Craig was also a friend of Marcus's. I just remember the bout being good for the local crowd with some action until I was able to stop Marcus in round 3.

FIGHT #49
06-28-2002 Otis Tisdale WBF Heavyweight Champ, St. Joseph, Missouri W KO 11
Won WBF Intercontinental Heavyweight Title

We promoted this next Fight with my new promotional company, All American Promotions. We brought Otis 'The Assassin' Tisdale in from Charlotte, NC. Tisdale said he was from New Jersey and acted out the part of being a bad ass East Coast Fighter who felt disrespected that he was even wasting his time coming to Missouri to fight a 'home-town kid.' He talked the fight up to his whole team, our whole city, and to me. I told him I already knew he was trying to make himself believe all the bullshit because I was not falling for the Banana in the Tail Pipe. Seriously though. He had already signed for a nice five-figure payday with no TV, so I was really glad he talked so much shit on television, as our country TV put him on as often as possible because he made so many people believe him that I was a blown up white boy who could not fight. One of the friends he made became members of my health club, Team Calloway, and told me all about him coming over to their house, as they were nice people who really did not know me well at the time either. Later they told me he came over and said he has done this several times where the media blows up the white fighter and people think he is a killer. Then they stepped him up too soon with me and I knocked out his ass. He never quit talking shit so we made sure he was on TV for interviews or at the radio station or doing an article for the newspaper. Not to be disrespectful to the people he was telling, but it's a known fact people wanna believe no one from their hometown can be as good as someone from the East Coast or West Coast it seems. Please forgive me if I offend anyone, as I'm not saying 100% of the people, I'm saying MOST. For instance, we sold more tickets for that fight than any other and in my opinion, it is because Tisdale made everyone believe his bullshit that he was a

117

Real Nigga that could fight and has fought Real Killas, he said. What he did not know was my life or background or the angry determination I had to be somebody one day and the way I felt about the Boxing Ring, that it was All on Me and I could not blame someone else for my failures. AND THAT IS THE WAY I LIKED IT. GO AHEAD AND BRING IT, OTIS 'THE ASSASSIN' TISDALE because you don't know me or anything about me, where I came from, how hard I worked to get where I'm at, or how hard I'm willing to work to get where I'm going.

We packed the arena and he bitched about everything. He got paid TV money for the fight but complained we were fighting in my ring. I said, "Cause it's a 16 X 16 foot ring and you said I would run and you would beat me up, bust me up and when you get tired of looking at me you was going to knock me out, so I wanted to make it easy for you and fight in my small ring instead of a 20 x 20 foot ring." I knew he didn't believe all the shit he was saying or he would have been excited about the 16 x 16 small ring. He also said I fought nothing but BUMs. I knew I had not and although he believed they were not his caliber, but some were very good fighters and looking at my record, I had knocked out most. So if they were not up to his level, I did not let them go the distance and if they did, I made sure everyone knew who the winner was, including my opponent.

Otis Tisdale continued to talk shit and not only had people believe he was going to show everyone I was blown up by local media just as some had wondered, all wanted to get a live seat to see what would happen. We moved the Weigh-Ins to the MALL and invited the public to attend and people packed the mall to see this man from the East Coast who was talking so much shit. Plus he was coming off a win on ESPN, making it even more believable what he was saying as I watched the fight and got it on tape and studied it each night.

This would be one of my favorite fights of long career as I have to admit he got to me a lot as well but not so much that I did not plan on whipping his ass and making him REMEMBER ME FOR THE REST OF HIS LIFE. I TOLD TISDALE AND THE MEDIA NOT TO

118

SOUND DISRESPECTFUL BECAUSE I WAS NOT ONLY GOING TO BEAT THE HELL OUT OF HIM, I WAS NOT GOING TO KNOCK HIM OUT UNTIL AS LATE AS POSSIBLE IN THE FIGHT SO HE WOULD HAVE ALL THE LUMPS AND BRUISES TO REMEMBER ME BY FOR TALKING SO MUCH BULLSHIT AND SCARING MY WIFE SO MUCH. Robin Rae would not let Chase go to the fight as she had seen him get emotional when watching Tisdale on TV talking about beating me and knocking me out etc. I never let butter go the fights until much later. I AM WHAT I AM, NO EXCUSES. GET GOOD AT MAKING EXCUSES, IT'S DIFFICULT TO EXCEL AT ANYTHING ELSE.

I loved seeing the new faces in the crowd and was feeling great, in shape, no partying, Nothing But Business. From Round One, I could see I was the better athlete with my left jab busting him up and my good movement setting up the left hook, right hand; body shots were coming together and soon I began to control the fight with my left jab, not running but moving precisely to set up different punches and I stayed busy putting him on the defensive. I could see his frustration building and felt sooner or later he was going to suck it up and go for it, so I just kept peppering him with the hard left jab, busting up his lips, nose, and every time he put his head down, I would push him a little with my glove just to piss him off. When he began to complain to the ref, I knew it was bothering him so I said, "Tell him to keep his head up." He really had the right to bob up and down but I just wanted to make the ref think he was doing just as much bullshit to me.

Soon he began to get really pissed and brought several hard blows and even hit me with his shoulder to my face so I thought OK, and either later in the round or it may have been the next, we got tied up after a combination and his shoulder was bumping my mouth so I bit him and the Ref did not see it as he was on the other side. I saw how pissed Tisdale was, and he began looking for the Ref to do something, BUT LET ME DEFINE AS I HAD MY MOUTHPIECE IN, HE JUST FELT ME BITE DOWN ON HIS SHOULDER WITH MY MOUTH GUARD, WHICH DID NOT CAUSE ANY PAIN; HE WAS JUST

BEING A BITCH. I went back to controlling with my jab and short combinations and I thought he had one or two more good flurries and the fight was getting late. Sure enough, in Round 8 he put together his Last Hurrah. I thought and I knew he did too that if he got to the twelfth he would make himself believe he could bring it hard as he could those last 3 minutes. So believe it or not—as it is hard to believe so many thoughts are going through my head in a Title Fight and the biggest fight in my hometown in my home arena—I do remember thinking I was going to really pick it up in the tenth round and if I did not get him then I was going to Knock His Ass Out in the eleventh.

I PICKED UP THE FIGHT, IMMEDIATELY LANDING THE SHOTS I WANTED AND ESPECIALLY THE RIGHT HAND WHICH STUNNED HIM AS HE WAS HURT AND TIRED AND NOBODY KNEW IT AS WELL AS I DID. HE WAS GOING DOWN BUT FALLING SLOWLY, SO I BROUGHT A LEFT HOOK-UPPERCUT ON HIS WAY DOWN THAT LEFT HIM LYING ON THE CANVAS DURING MOST OF OUR VICTORY CELEBRATION. ONE OF MY FAVORITE FIGHTS AS I HAD PROVEN TO MYSELF AND FAMILY WITH WINS OVER ALL THE MIDWEST GUYS AND THEN BEAT DOMINIC CARTER, DARYL SPINKS, TROY WEIDA NEAR HIS HOMETOWN IN ILLINOIS. BUT STILL SO MANY PEOPLE DID NOT WANT TO GET ON THE BANDWAGON UNTIL AFTER THIS FIGHT AND MANY STILL DID NOT AS YOU CAN NEVER MAKE EVERYONE LIKE YOU. I KNEW AND UNDERSTOOD THIS AND WAS OK WITH IT.

I MUST SAY EVERY TIME I WATCH THIS FIGHT, I HAVE TO WATCH IT ALL SO I CAN SEE MY BEAUTIFUL WIFE JUMP AROUND IN THE RING AND WAVE UP TO THE CROWD, FEELING SO GOOD, SO HAPPY, AND SHOWING SO MUCH LOVE FOR HER HUSBAND WHO SHE HAS SACRIFICED SO MUCH FOR, ALWAYS SUPPORTING MY DREAM OF BEING WORLD CHAMPION. I sometimes watch the film of the fight and remember his manager calling my promoter, my brother-in-law, who was working for me and told me as soon as he hung up that Otis was mad at them, meaning him, the manager, and his head trainer, and was not paying them.

IF YOU GET A CHANCE, WATCH THE CALLOWAY-TISDALE FIGHT ON YOUTUBE AND KEEP WATCHING THE CELEBRATION UNTIL THE BEAUTIFUL BRUNETTE JUMPS UP AND DOWN IN THE RING, CRYING HAPPY TEARS AND WAVING HER ARMS TO HER HOMETOWN CROWD, LOVING HER HUSBAND!!!

I was feeling very good at this time of my life. I had an international title, bringing Tisdale to town and knocking him out in the eleventh round after telling everybody I wanted and planned to knock him out late in the fight so he will always remember my name. I think about the things I would say or do like at press conferences, throwing water bottles, yelling, but that is just me. I do have a little problem. Boxing was good for me. I think sometimes I needed boxing. I get sad and mad at myself nowadays as I know my son would never get mad and act like a crazy person, yelling or throwing stuff at opponent, and many judge him as he is my son—My Pride and Joy—I loved him boxing as a kid, but I hate and never thought he would be judged by my actions. You know what I mean—Chase is Better than me! I know this as he throws correct punches at the correct times and I never started until 19 years old. Anyway, I love my son and look forward to watching Chase continue to be the best man he can be which will always be Great to his Dad and his Mom. Neither Robin nor I care about how much longer you can box, just so you love the competition of the toughest sport in the world and you're always in shape so you never take too many unnecessary punches.

FIGHT #50
09-08-2002 Eric Davis, Ramada Inn, St. Joseph, MO
W KO 9

My next fight would be #50 and we even put together a cheesy commercial for our local TV with me wearing a tuxedo with boxing gloves saying come to watch my 50th bout at the Ramada Inn Ball Room.

We had just sold out the arena and now we put on a fight in this little ballroom, however I was as well known at this time as anyone in the city, if not the most well known athlete, so my team put 50 round tables of 10 seats and sold tickets for $1,000 per table. When I say team, I mean my beautiful wife Robin Rae Redmond Calloway. The tables sold out in few weeks, and she had worked out a dinner as well as a bottle of champagne for each table. My wife is the salesman in the family. Again she reminds me I could not sell a glass of water in hell. I LOVE HER MORE EVERY YEAR, MONTH, WEEK, AND DAY, THOUGH.

I beat a man who I had beaten before, but he was able to go the distance with me at one of the casinos in Kansas City and he also was a southpaw. I not only wanted to win but WIN BY KNOCKOUT. I MAY HAVE STILL HAD A LITTLE PROBLEM.

FIGHT #51
10-05-2002 Ruslan Chagaev 2x Heavyweight WBA Champ, Cobo Hall, Detroit, Michigan TD 3

Many watched live on Showtime Championship Boxing.

Ruslan 'White Tyson' Chagaev was a 2-time World Amateur Champion and did not have many professional fights but was beating everybody up in sparring. I was told a couple years earlier from the trainer Kenny Adams, who worked with me some before my world title fight with Keene, that soon I would hear of a guy from Russia who will be the Heavyweight Champion of the World. Kenny said, "His name is Ruslan Chagaev. He can punch like a damn champ and has great boxing skills to go along with his southpaw style." I'm glad I got this fight for so many reasons:

— People got to see that I'm a real fighter. I never quit or take the easy way out. Chagaev landed some huge blows and I soon was seriously out on my feet but just refused to go down. Thank GOD the ref correctly called the head butt that caused the cut over my eye. After the doctor asked if I could continue, I said, "Yes" until he was forced to stop it due to the deep cut that required several stitches to get closed up at the Detroit Emergency Room hours after the fight.

— I showed myself, my family and friends, and anybody who may have doubted before that I will never quit in a fight and that I'm there to Win 100%, never coming for just a payday.

— I also got a chance to fight in front of my friend, Marshall Mathers, otherwise known as Eminem, who was nice enough to allow us to come to his house and to his studio, 9 Mile Studio, and introduced me to his friend and co-star in the movie 8 Mile, Mekhi Phifer. Eminem had called Mekhi up and asked him if he wanted to fly to Detroit from LA and go to the Showtime Fights to watch one of Eminem's homeboys from St. Joseph, Missouri fighting in the co-main event.

Back in 1998, I had taken Chase when he was just 3 years old with me when I was asked to be a speaker for 'Time For Two,' a project put together to get men to be more involved with their small children. I agreed if I could bring Chase even though the class was for 5 and 6 year olds who have not started the first grade yet. I remember the ladies who helped put this event together being so impressed with Chase at just 3 years old being at the reading level he was at and so happy to join in during discussions and playing a role as a 1st grader during the time he was with the kids while the dads had their time together to speak about different ideas each had or just share about their time with their kids.

One of the reasons I loved the experience was one of the dads who brought his kids to class, Jack, said his wife had a nephew who was a fight fan of mine too and he had won a rap contest to go to California to rap in the national contest and the winner would get a contract with DR. DRE.

I said I had heard about his nephew from guys around the boxing gym, who said he was the real deal and Jack said, "We'll see. I think so too, but it's a tough game just like boxing in a way." THAT KID HE WAS SPEAKING ABOUT WAS MARSHALL MATHERS, ALSO KNOWN AS EMINEM. I REMEMBER JACK TELLING ME HE SPELLS IT DIFFERENTLY. WOW. HOW AWESOME TO RUN INTO JACK AND FOLLOW EM IN HIS ENTIRE CAREER AND TO HAVE AN OPPORTUNITY TO GO TO HIS HOME, TO HIS STUDIO ON 9 MILE, MEET MEKHI PHIFER WHO EM INVITED

TO COME TO THE FIGHT. AND OF COURSE HE DID AND SAT RINGSIDE AT THE JOE LOUIS ARENA IN DETROIT MICHIGAN WHERE I FOUGHT THE SOON HEAVYWEIGHT CHAMPION OF THE WORLD AND ALREADY A 2X AMATEUR WORLD CHAMPION.

I boxed aggressively as I only know how to and won the first round on the scorecards. In the second round, I continued doing well again until we both threw big punches, my right and his left, and both of us missing but clashing heads, leaving mine a bloody mess. After the doctor first looked at it, I said, "I'm fine and want to continue." Ruslan saw the blood and was bringing big punches and I refused to go down. I remember feeling the hot blood pouring off my face but I also felt I was in a good fight in front of my family, cornermen, and all the people around the US watching on Showtime, so I would never allow myself to quit or think I was not going to win somehow. I have said Hasim 'Rock' Rahman hits harder than any opponent I have fought in my career, but I will say Ruslan 'White Tyson' Chagaev hits the hardest with his left hand. He's a huge puncher and I'm glad for him and his family that he won the WBA World Heavyweight Championship in Russia versus the 7'0 tall Russian, Nikolai Valuev, after our rematch in Germany. I always thought Ruslan would beat

Klitschko as well however he was beaten in their World Title Unification match in Germany.

I fought in Germany years later, when I was fighting for the money, the attention, and the love of boxing after I knew I was finished as a contender in the sport, the game that keeps so many fighting too long, not listening to themselves or others close to them to quit. I love my wife for telling me. I remember walking across the arena floor to say hello to Ruslan Chagaev. He was talking to someone else at the time so did not see me coming. It's hard to believe how popular we get in the sport of boxing among real boxing fans all over the world as it seemed the whole arena of 20 thousand people were watching me walk over to him with his back turned. His wife saw me coming and once I got to the stage, started tapping Ruslan on shoulder. She tapped harder and faster the closer I got until he turned to her and yelled, "WHAT?" She just pointed to me and Ruslan started taking a few steps in my direction. I stuck my hand out for him and he shook it and gave me a hug. I asked him to take a picture with me and I had my brother-in-law Jason use his phone camera, but I never received a copy to this day for my book. I heard Ruslan speaking about me through translation prior to my fight and I was very happy to earn his respect as a fighter in the ring. I thank him for the kind words and I will always be a fan.

Thanks, Champ, Ruslan White Tyson Chagaev, ONE OF TWO MEN TO KNOCK ME 'OUT' IN 92 PROFESSIONAL FIGHTS.

I've mentioned I enjoyed driving around on Sunday and looking at houses with Robin and the kids as Riley Rae 'Butter' would always fall asleep soon as I backed out of the driveway.

We had a cute little house when we got married but I soon wanted another and then after our kids came, after I had a fight on Showtime, I took the money and took Robin a few miles from our current home to see a house being built in Carriage Oaks. I told her, "We can make changes now or additions or whatever you want and it's four stories, Robin. Kids have their own basement and we can have ours plus a three-car garage and huge back yard and it's everything you want."

She said, "Everything you want. I'm happy where we are." Well, I told you she is always right.

Little quick story:

Big Daddy told Riley Rae one time when she was around 2 years old, "Nobody is right all the time, Riley."

She said, "Uh huh."

Big Daddy said, "Who???"

Riley Rae said, "MY MOMMA!"

Well, I do not have to tell you that Riley Rae got whatever she wanted from her Grandpa after that comment—after he laughed his ass off for a little while and dried the tears from his eyes.

FIGHT #52
10-25-2002 Jason Nicholson, Ultimate Fighting Champ from Oklahoma City, OK, Lakeside Casino, Osceola, Iowa W PTS 6

I fought Jason Nicholson again and this time at the Lakeside Casino in Iowa. I know I should have not taken this bout with my head having a bad cut just 20 days before, but the commission and doctor all said Ok so it was ON. I felt comfortable as I felt Nicholson's style was made to order for me so I just stayed outside and controlled the fight with my left jab, winning a unanimous decision.

FIGHT #53
02-08-2003 Audley Harrison, 2000 Super Heavyweight Olympic Champ, Brentford Fountain Leisure Centre, London, England L TKO 4 6 Many viewed on the BBC Television Network

I remember this fight for several reasons. One, I took my wife Robin Rae Calloway with me to London and she got to see a different part of the world, which just made me feel good even though she never ask to go. Now that I'm thinking about it, I'm not sure she even wanted to go, but she did go and Jason's wife Natalie went along with her as well, keeping her company on the long plane ride as well as watching me fight the 2000 Super Heavyweight Olympic Gold Medalist of the Sydney Olympics in Australia.

I trained hard and brought the fight to Audley and really thought I would win, however he threw a left uppercut and landed it right beneath my right jawbone. I immediately felt it break. I made it through the round and when I went back to the corner, I said take the mouthpiece out, as I had to puke with so much blood in mouth. Thank God the doctors saw the mess in the corner and stopped the fight. I was offered free health care in England, but the hospital looked like a 1930's movie and after talking to Robin, I said, "Let's just wait until we get home and have a local doctor fix it."

Years later, I became friends with a guy from Liverpool, England named David. He was a fan of mine and was at the fight with Audley in England and said I was winning and he was sorry I got caught with the wild left uppercut. He even spoke to my wife on our way out of the arena and was very nice, which I appreciated. I became more impressed with David as he even stuck up for me on a local website put on from some cross-town rivals. Well, David and I were right, and he has always been a good boxing fan of mine. He respected my toughness and the fact I always fought my very best, win or lose, and always brought 100%. I want to say it has been very nice to have a friend from England named David Lucockand. I hope we can meet one day but if we never do, I have always appreciated you being a fan and friend to the All American Prize Fighter. I always did the best I could do, David, and having friends like you has made it worth it. Thanks Champ!!!

I did not like the food in England and it was a good thing I guess, as I did not eat but just drank everything I could until we got back. My friends and Cornermen got everything set up so when I got back I met with a doctor, Dr. Don Gosset, who knew who I was from all the publicity from local media. Doc was also a friend of ours from our church, What Park Baptist, the new one close to our home now.

Doc met us at his office that night after we returned from England to look at X-rays and set up an appointment for the next morning. He gave me wires on top and bottom to hold mouth shut. That worked pretty well for a couple of days, but I was gritting my teeth and was bothered with the wires in my mouth, so I soon broke them and we needed to call the Doc to take a look. This time he put in staples and more wires, making sure I would not break them again. This time I was a few weeks into it but getting bored and began playing basketball at Team Calloway, our Family Health and Fitness Club.

I had two awesome goals with extra large fiberglass backboards and we all got so much great use out of those9-foot basketball goals on the Team Calloway Court, which is the level they remained at so we could all feel bigger. Every Year we would have the 9-foot 3-on-3 dunk tournament that I like to say became famous around St. Joseph during our Anniversary Celebration every summer. I became friends with so many great guys who liked boxing and following my career that I sometimes forget to think of them as celebrities and just enjoy being able to call them my friends.

Well, one day I was outside playing basketball in the middle of the day as we were always slow over lunchtime, and broke my jaw again while dunking the ball. Doc fixed my jaw again with screws, plates, and wires up around my nose bone to keep my mouth shut and told me, "No more basketball!" and I don't have to tell everyone Robin was getting tired of telling me as well.

The break was February 8th, 2003 and after the mess, I went through with the broken jaw being wired and in surgery three different times to redo the broken wires from gritting teeth or playing basketball, running, and jumping, I was finally forced to be safe and be still, which drove me crazy. I will say the most fun about the broken jaw was my baby Riley Rae would soon become less scared of her daddy speaking through the wires and each night it became a regular on both of our schedules for her to pick out a few books and come and sit on my knee for me to read. I found I could relax and speak with my mouth barely opened pretty well and loved reading books to Butter. *Through The Wires*—GREAT SONG.

We had such great kids at this time—not that they have not always been, but at this time we all loved Coleman Elementary School and the teachers, principal, and the other parents.

Chase had not had his first boxing match yet and we never thought about him becoming Kid Dynamite at this time.

I was blessed to not only have an awesome doctor who fixed my jaw back to normal but do it all without charging me when he could have and probably should with all the trouble I caused with repeating the break on three occasions, because he knew I didn't have health insurance. I love you, Doctor Don Gossett! I feel so blessed to have met a friend for life and having you in my life meant a lot to my wife and me as well. I was honored you came to my fights so many times and carried out one of my championship belts prior to me entering the ring, which became a tradition prior to my bouts at home. It was always an honor for me to have a respected man like yourself carry one to the ring and be in my corner and be my friend. Thank you, Doctor Gosset. Robin and I love you.

I'm not sure Doctor Gosset was too happy about it, but we soon announced my next fight would be in St. Joseph, Missouri and would be against a 7'1" tall fighter from Detroit. His father and uncle were professional basketball players and although he excelled in that sport as well, he took up boxing and soon began to make a name for himself, being such a big man. I remember making the contracts and him signing to come into town early to sharpen up before the fight for the media, including our local television station KQ2, our local radio station KJO, and our local newspaper the Newspress.

FIGHT #54
10-18-2003 Julius Long, St. Joseph, Missouri W UD 12
WBF Intercontinental Heavyweight Title Defense

A few years later, setting up for a fight down town at the Civic Arena, Galen Brown said the reason so many people came to see that fight was to see me get my ass kicked.

I told Galen, "Well, I'm GLAD THEY CAME AND PAID TO GET IN AND I'M GLAD THEY SAW ME KICK HIS ASS FOR 12 ROUNDS."

I realize he was telling me the truth as few years later when Galen and I fought, I got to see the true colors of many who were cheering for Galen Brown to win. I feel everyone wants to see a good fight and that's what they pay to see, but several of his fans, people, just mad cause they been misled, thinking he was better than ME or he was close to being as good as me just because he was better than some other local bums—I hate to call fighters bums, I really do, but who I'm talking about I don't even consider real fighters. See how pissed I get still just by thinking about our fight... STAY TUNED!!!

Julius and I had a good fight and his only problem was although he was 7'0 tall, he did not use his jab, the most important punch in boxing, in my opinion. I would outjab him, trying to make sure I would throw two or three at a time to get me close enough to throw my right hand and hook. I know he was 7'0 tall but his neck was only about 6'0, and I tried to hit him in his Adams apple all night and did a couple of occasions. But he never quit and was really a lot tougher than I had given him credit for being. No disrespect as I had seen him fight before and I just felt a lot of people would want to come and see it in St. Joseph, so we made the fight happen. I realized later I was crazy as I was coming off a broken jaw from my England fight and this bout was only 6 months later. Well I did box well and used my jab often and with education, meaning throwing at the right time and double and tripling up when necessary. I also landed a right hand that shook him and he retreated safely, but I felt good about being able to shake such a big man with my right hand punch, again letting me know I can really crack. I always will remember my family coming out for this fight and one of the family members that came was a good fighter and loved the sport of boxing as well. I just remember when I was in the ring in my corner and I looked down at Robin at ringside before the fight started as I usually always do, but this time I looked down the row and remember seeing my uncle so nervous. He had a nervous laugh he could not control. I know he was scared for me even though he had seen me fight and win so many fights on ESPN, as we always let family back home in Kentucky know when we were fighting on TV. Julius Long vs. me was a good fight for me since I won 9 of the 12 rounds on all three judges' scorecards, retaining my WBF Title.

FIGHT #55
12-27-2003 Jason Nicholson Ultimate Fighting Champ, St. Joseph, Missouri W KO 3
WBF Intercontinental Heavyweight Title Defense

This was a fight with Nicholson when I did not agree to just win every round so he could go the distance and fight again soon afterwards. I told him and his trainer George Clarke, who are actually both now friends, that I was going to knock him out, so go ahead and keep talking and be ready to bring it, cause I am!!! 100%

I came out boxing with a hard left jab as I did not want to walk into anything unnecessary, so I won the first round easily, controlling with my left jab and dropping the right hand few times. In the second round, I was slowing him down with the number of punches I was putting together and landing until I had Jason in my corner where I really set up to land one of my best right hands. I kept touching him with my left hand, moving over slightly to my left to set up the right hand and then brought an overhand right, hitting him right on the top of nose, leaving blood everywhere. BUT Jason Nicholson took it and would not go down but just leaned back on the ropes. The bell rang and he slowly stumbled back to his corner. I sat down and thought *holy shit, I really thought I knocked his BRAINS OUT with that last right hand.* Well, thank GOD he did not come out for the third round and I thank his trainer and cornerman, George Clarke, for stopping the fight in the corner. Jason is another guy who remains friends still today with my family and me. HE IS ONE TOUGH SOB.

FIGHT #56
3-12-04 Dino Salcedo, St. Joseph, Missouri W KO 2

Dino was a good guy from Omaha, Nebraska who was a tough wrestler and football player in high school and even made a name for himself in the MMA business, but I felt comfortable with his size in the ring as a boxer and was able to outbox him for first round and half of the next before putting together some good combinations and landing a knockout punch late in the 2nd round.

FIGHT #57
5-26-04 Jeff Ford, Ameristar Casino, Kansas City, Missouri
W KO 2

I still did not feel I was getting the respect I deserved around the Midwest from other fighters and some of the fans. The talk around the Midwest was about the big upset of an up-and-coming heavyweight, Ty Fields, who was a very big, muscular guy and had lots of power and looked the part as well, but after being built up from the KC media he was knocked out at the Ameristar Casino in Kansas City by Jeff Ford from Kansas City. We wanted to step up again, so we contacted Ford's people to get the bout made for the end of May at the same casino where he had upset Fields.

The bout was a huge success as people were beginning to know me as well as hearing about Ford's big upset with his powerful right hand punch, and the place was sold out, including many Kansas City Chiefs football players and Kansas City Royals baseball players sitting ringside in the VIP section. I got myself in great shape, expecting a tough fight however I was able to land some clean shots early in the second round including my left hook-right hand combination that put Ford to sleep in front of Tony Gonzales and Jason Dunn. They came back to my locker room after the fight and even invited my wife Robin and me to come and eat dinner with the team after the impressive win.

I remember everyone being nice and liking a winner, of course, but I mainly remember meeting a guy who would become one of my best friends amongst the professional athletes in the game of football, JASON DUNN, A BIG TIGHT END WHO WAS AN OUTSTAND-ING BLOCKER WITH GOOD HANDS AT TIMES AS WELL. THE GREAT THING WAS JASON CAME UP TO ME AS OUR MU-TUAL FRIEND D-SPICE TOLD HIM I WAS FROM KENTUCKY AND SAID, "MAN, THERE ARE ALWAYS KENTUCKY GUYS COMING OUT OF THE WOODWORK." JASON WAS FROM SHELBYVILLE, KENTUCKY CLOSE TO LOUISVILLE, KEN-TUCKY AND MY MOTHER WAS LIVING IN THAT AREA T THAT TIME. IN FACT, ONE DAY FEW YEARS LATER, I GOT A

CALL FROM MY MOM WHO WAS WORKING HER 2ND JOB AT A CONVENIENCE STORE AND SHE SAID, "GUESS WHO I SAW TONIGHT?" I SAID, "I HAVE NO IDEA." SHE SAID, "A TALL BLACK MAN WITH LONG HAIR CAME IN WITH SOME FRIENDS AND I TOLD HIM I HAVE TO ASK, DO YOU KNOW ROB CALLOWAY AND HE SAID YES I DO, HE IS MY FRIEND FROM KANSAS CITY AND A GREAT FIGHTER." MOM SAID, "THAT IS MY SON AND HE HAS SENT ME PICS OF YOU TWO AND ALWAYS SPOKE HIGHLY OF YOU." MOM SAID JASON WALKED RIGHT AROUND THE COUNTER AND GAVE HER A BIG HUG AND AS I HAVE SAID BEFORE, I FEEL BLESSED TO HAVE TOUCHED SO MANY PEOPLE AND MANY WHO I AM A BIG FAN OF LIKE JASON DUNN. LOVE TO FEEL LOVE FROM REAL MEN WHO KNOW WHAT WORKING HARD TO BECOME THE BEST YOU CAN BE IN A SPORT RESPECTED BY SO MANY. JASON IS FROM A TOWN ONLY HOURS FROM WHERE I LIVED MUCH OF MY YEARS AS A TEEN. HE EVEN FLEW OUT TO WATCH ME FIGHT MY NEXT FIGHT AND THEN WAS MAN ENOUGH TO WALK OUT WITH ME FROM THE LOCKER ROOM TO THE RING WHEN I FOUGHT THE FORMER HEAVYWEIGHT CHAMPION OF THE WORLD, HA-SIM THE ROCK RAHMAN IN BALTIMORE, MARYLAND.

YEARS LATER, OF COURSE, ROCK AND I BECAME GOOD FRIENDS AND WE STILL KEEP IN TOUCH TO THIS DAY. I FELT GREAT TO BE ABLE TO TELL JASON DUNN ABOUT ROCK ASKING ABOUT THE KC CHIEF FOOTBALL PLAYERS WHO FLEW OUT TO SEE US FIGHT IN BALTIMORE. OF COURSE, I TELL THE CHAMP ALL WAS GOING WELL UNTIL YOU HAD TO LAND THAT LUCKY PUNCH. ROCK LAUGHS TOO.

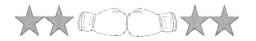

FIGHT #58
6-17-04 Hasim Rahman Former Heavyweight Champion of the World, Michael's Eighth Avenue, Glen Burnie, Maryland
L KO 2

My fight with Rock was memorable for me as he was the first World Heavyweight Champion I got in the ring with. Rock was a real fighter and I respect him not only because he was the biggest puncher I ever fought but because he was real man who after the fight came into my locker room and said, "Rob, you're one hell of a puncher and you caught me with a great punch. I'm serious, you're one of the top 5 or 6 punchers I have ever fought." I said, "Damn. Thank you for coming in and telling me that, Champ, and since we're talking about punching power, I want to tell you that you are the biggest puncher I have ever fought and I can't believe a man can hit so hard." Years later while doing interview on ESPN, I was asked who was the biggest puncher and I said,"Rock with right hand and Chagaev with his left as they

137

were the only two to beat me by KNOCKOUT." The guy doing the interview said I told him Chagaev was biggest puncher so several months later, when Rock and I were at camp together, he hit me in the stomach with a big right hand during one of our sparring rounds just to let me know who was biggest puncher. There was only a few seconds left in the round so I just got as close as I could to him so he couldn't hit me again until the bell rang. I said, "Damn you, Rock!!!"

He had a good laugh but I will say Hasim 'Rock' Rahman is the Biggest Puncher I fought in 92 Professional Fights.

FIGHT #59
10-8-04 Kerry Biles, Lakeside Casino, Osceola, Iowa W KO 4
Mid-American Heavyweight Title

My next bout was back in Iowa at a casino I had fought at before and was treated well. It was close to my home I always enjoyed being able to fight close. Our local media was always very nice and I felt very fortunate to be able to share the fight with all the local people around St. Joseph, Missouri either by the local television station KQ2, the local radio station of KJO 105, and/or our local paper the St. Joseph News Press. All three were always great about giving me my share of press from the announcement of the bout being made until weeks after the final bell.

FIGHT #60
10-29-04 Andy Sample, St. Joseph, Missouri W KO 2
WBF Intercontinental Heavyweight Title Defense

My 60th bout was against a guy from Topeka, Kansas who was a good amateur and had a good professional career with a good record. He brought several fans from Topeka to see if he had what it took to beat me in my hometown of St. Joseph, as many from Topeka had heard of me, and many boxing people from St. Joseph had heard of Sample, as we were only around 75 miles from each other.

I defended the Intercontinental Title I had won from Tisdale. I admit Andy was good boxer with some boxing skill, but I was too strong, aggressive, meaner, and wanted to win the fight much more than he did and still had goals of being world champion and not just happy with being a good local fighter, which I thought he was ok with.

FIGHT #61
12-3-04 Jeff Pegues, Municipal Auditorium, Kansas City, Missouri
W KO 2

We began to have a lot of fans from Kansas City as well and a local promoter put on a show at the Municipal Auditorium, inviting many athletes from the KC area, including Chiefs and Royals. I felt he was the best promoter around the area at this time and we worked out deal for several fights. I really enjoyed fighting on Joe Kelly's cards and he always treated me fairly. I remember Pegues was a former professional football player for the Washington Redskins and Cleveland Browns, but although he was strong, I was much faster and could box and punch and was able to get him out of there in just two rounds, giving me an opportunity to look impressive in front of the nice Kansas City crowd.

FIGHT #62
1-26-05 Kerry Biles, Ameristar Casino, Kansas City, Missouri
W KO 6

I was back in the ring again at the Ameristar casino just over a month later versus another big heavyweight again with less skill than I had. I always had punching power that allowed me to even compete with big heavyweights. I loved to hit people hard in the ring and especially the big heavyweights. Even with my jab, I was able to let my opponents know I had power and always fought aggressively, always being in good shape and wanting to pressure my opponent until they got tired, and always wanted to win by KNOCKOUT.

FIGHT #63
2-5-05 Travis Fulton, The Digz, Omaha Nebraska W KO 1

I remember this fight being in a cool arena, although old, but also because it was promoted by a former opponent and he put me up against a guy who was tough fighter and tough MMA guy as well. I landed some great shots, but I think the fight was stopped too early as Fulton was a tough SOB who would always come to fight.

FIGHT #64
3-4-05 Daniel Frank, South American Heavyweight Champion, St. Joseph, Missouri W KO 1

I remember this bout as we brought in a guy from Sao Paulo, Brazil and we had a great crowd. I loved this fight for couple of reasons: First, Tony 'TNT' Tubbs was a mutual friend of mine and Clint

Calkins, a fighter/manager/trainer from Iowa who asked if Tony could get on our upcoming card at the arena in St. Joseph, so I said sure. Also Tony came into our locker room and held punch mitts and had me throwing my overhand right instead of just the straight right hand and we worked on it for over 30 minutes in the locker room before the bout. He was even awesome enough to walk out with my corner people and me and agreed to work the corner. I've been a fan of Tubbs for as long as I could remember and I felt really great to have the champ teaching me stuff in the locker room and even agreeing to work my corner. Tony was good guy, who got caught up with the bad part of boxing that took much of his money along with his weakness to drugs, but he was a real fighter and knew so much about the sport of boxing, I think he could be a great trainer for someone still. I remember boxing the big Brazilian, using my jab, staying half a man but setting up for my overhand right that Tony 'TNT' Tubbs and I had been just working on. I put my opponent in the perfect position and I came over as hard and fast as I could. THE WHOLE ARENA 'HEARD' THE PUNCH IF THEY DID NOT SEE IT AND I WON BY A PRETTY BIG UP-SET, WINNING SO EARLY BY KNOCKOUT. I REMEMBER TONY RUNNING INTO THE RING AND PICKING ME UP AND I WILL SAY THIS IS ANOTHER OF MY FAVORITE MEMORIES FROM MY LONG CAREER AS IT SURE FELT GREAT TO HAVE THE FORMER WORLD HEAVYWEIGHT CHAMPION TONY 'TNT' TUBBS TEACH ME SOMETHING AND THEN FOR ME TO PUT THE INSTRUCTION TO USE IN SUCH A BIG WAY. THANKS CHAMP!!!

I was able to use this fight to help raise a little money for Former Heavyweight Champion Greg Page, who was the fighter I had heard so much about as a kid from Kentucky. I had this fight in St. Joseph, Missouri, our home, to help pay some bills for his family. One of my greatest memories was taking my wife and kids to meet the Champ and his wife in Louisville prior to a visit to see my mother. I remember asking Greg, "Do you remember me, as in 1994 I had my first fight in Las Vegas and you was the trainer of the fighter I knocked out? He was from Jamaica but lived and trained in Vegas with you." The Champ said, "You knocked the hell out of my boy. I remember that." His wife was so happy and said, "He can remember things years ago easy but can't remember what he did 10 minutes ago." Greg's short-term memory was terrible. I did a charity bout to raise money for his family after Greg was injured in the ring and that is one of my greatest boxing moments when I got to bring my family to meet his family and give his wife a little money to help with medical expenses. There was another great fighter I admired for his outstanding skill named Gerald McClellan and my charity fight was also to raise money for Gerald as well as Greg. Gerald's sister was his caretaker and told me after the Bout at our St. Joseph Civic Arena as she brought Gerald to watch my bout to give her portion of the money to Greg and his wife as well because Roy Jones, Jr. had just given them money for expenses and she wanted Patricia Page to have it. The graciousness of her to think of Greg and Patricia was awesome but also the fact that Roy Jones was giving her money made me cry, as boxing is full of so many great people, I have come to learn over the years. I never met Roy but hope to one day, as he is one of my favorite boxers and one of my favorite people as well after hearing the story from Gerald's sister.

FIGHT #65
5-14-05 Jim Strohl, NABC World Heavyweight Title, Delta Center, Salt Lake City, Utah W KO 6

Well the last fight was great and exciting for the hometown crowd as so many talked about me landing that big punch to stop the Brazilian in just the first round. The fight also got attention down under as the President of the WBF gave us a call offering an opportunity to fight Big Bob Mirovic on the Gold Coast of Australia for the World

Heavyweight Championship. After getting a couple of calls from Chagaev Management wanting a rematch, as they felt he was seconds away from being awarded a win by knockout before the referee stepped in to call the bout a draw from the prior head butt that was continuing to bleed profusely from my forehead, but I would not quit and still kept throwing punches. I'm glad the ref stopped the bout so the doctor could take a look and the doctor did the right thing by stopping the bout, as I was not going to quit. I knew we would one day have a rematch and I did my job by continuing to win fights all around the USA and soon the world because I knew if I could win this bout in Salt Lake City, Utah and pick up another minor title to go along with my intercontinental belt, I would get a chance at the WBF World Heavyweight Title. I felt this would give me a great tool in negotiations for my rematch with Ruslan Chagaev in our rematch.

I continued to train hard everyday, eating right, sparring, all the weights and boxing training to be the best I could be and we even worked out a deal for us to come to Utah early so I could finish up training, including running and sparring up in the mountains of Park City, Utah, a ski resort town who had a local boxing gym with some locals on the undercard as well. All of this training was preparing me for this bout, which I knew I needed to win decisively so I could go on to Australia and have my opportunity at a world championship in Australia versus a guy who had been their best heavyweight that country had in the past 10 years. I hated being away from Robin and kids so long but I really thought these next few fights would put us in place to live a comfortable lifestyle for years to come.

My cornermen and friends who came along for the fight were there for me and soon as I was put to bed around 10:00 pm, they hit the town and I always thought of Salt Lake City, Utah of being a Mormon town with not much partying going on, but I soon saw I was definitely wrong about the Mormon population, as I can't remember a city that partied less.

Strohl brought the fight and had a Hall-of-Fame fighter in his corner, Mike 'The Bodysnatcher' McCallum, so I knew he was ready. I had kept winning impressively back home several fights prior to this one and getting fans from all around our area as well as making friends with many former great athletes, including Jason Sutherland who was a great basketball player for the University of Missouri and Alan Williams who was a great running back in Georgia and was drafted to play for the Detroit Lions back in the day when Barry Sanders was the Man, not only for the Lions but for the NFL where each game and every time he touched the ball was a highlight reel. Well, I was so happy Alan and Jason wanted to come out to Salt Lake City and be with me and my team for the fight. I remember the guys carrying my belts out at the Delta Center for the fight and how great it was for me to be able to fight in such an awesome arena and be the main event, having an opportunity to meet so many great athletes from the Salt Lake City area and then put on one of my best displays of boxing aggressively in the ring. I was feeling good and really felt my hard work for years was coming together with already signing for a world title fight in Australia as soon as I was successful in this one and I was not going to let Strohl get in my way of becoming the world champion!

I boxed aggressively and landed several big left hooks and right hands and was taking what he gave me from the body until, after continuing to apply the pressure, I landed a left hook/uppercut that I had been working on along with my big right hand to follow that stretched Strohl out in his own corner.

We celebrated and all I could think about was getting home to get my World Championship in Australia contract signed.

ROUND
9

FIGHT #66
6-24-05 Bob Mirovic, Royal Pines Resort, Ashmore, Gold Coast, Queensland, Australia W UD 12
WBF World Heavyweight Title and PABA Heavyweight Title

I returned from Salt Lake City, Utah after a good win versus Strohl who had one of my favorite boxers that I followed for years in the 90's as his head trainer, Mike 'The Bodysnatcher' McCallum. That was a great ring name as he was the Bodysnatcher. I actually knew Strohl a little as I believe he is originally from St. Louis Missouri. I was feeling good about my conditioning as I was set up by the promoter who I had met around a year earlier, Edward Mendy. Ed set up a training camp for us in Park City, Utah for a few weeks and I got myself in great shape prior to the fight. I had been speaking to an Australian promoter about an opportunity to fight for the World Heavyweight Championship in Australia as I had won the WBF International Championship and had been defending it regularly. The WBF President was interested in giving me the chance to fight for the World Title and we had our passports from fights in Denmark and England already. I felt all I needed was good sparring to finish off my preparation and to be as good as I was capable of making myself. I had my brother-in-law, Jason Redmond, as my head trainer and my best friend, Steve Ward, as my second who was even registered as my cut man, although he was our cable guy back home in St. Joseph. He was my best friend and a big sports fan and promoter of boxing matches and wrestling matches as well as being involved in sports of his own and coach of his girls' basketball games. I'm not sure how qualified he was to be in a world champion's corner but my brother-in-law and Steve both did a great job. I asked them to tell me who won the round after I got back to my corner and was able to breathe a little first and get my faced cleaned off and a drink of water. They both did a great job doing as I had asked, so in my opinion, I could not have asked for a better corner. My eye after round 8 became very swollen and was closing, however I was able to see out of it until the minute after round 11 and I told my brother to tell me how many fingers he was holding up so I would not get it wrong. I told him to pinch me on the side to tell me. Seriously. I remember him pinching me, but I had no idea how many times so I just mumbled two which is the number they usually do so I stayed with it.

I also had a friend of our family named Darwin who was a Native American that played football for a local Indian university. His uncles lived in St. Joseph and he had heard of me. When we met, we became friends and he wanted to learn more about boxing as his uncles were fans and they were former boxers as well. They had taught Darwin and felt he was pretty good and he was. Though around 320 pounds, he loved playing basketball and had some rhythm and was able to adapt to boxing. He worked for us at Team Calloway, our Family Health and

Fitness Club and opened up in the mornings for us awhile. I'm glad he got to experience a great time being my sparring partner for few months and was blessed to be able to have him go along with us to Australia and even be my sparring partner there, leading up to the fight. I remember the Australians really liked Darwin and he liked them as well. I even talked him into trying some vegemite, which is a yeast and vegetable food paste that people down under enjoy somehow. Darwin did not like it at all but we all had a good laugh one morning at breakfast. Robin was mad at me as, of course, she loved Darwin and he looked to her like a mother.

Jamie Myer was the promoter of the event and picked us up at the airport. I remember Jamie looking at me as I was a very small heavyweight and asked if I knew anything about Mirovic. I said, "We do not, but I understand he is a big heavyweight and I'm ready and prepared to fight and beat your champion." Jamie liked the confidence but I'm not sure he believed he was getting ready to promote the Fox Sports *Fight of the Year* and a fight still talked about now 10 years later on social media.

I remember Jamie driving us around the first few days and he had on a country music radio station. I said, "You like country?" He said, "Turn it to whatever you want, Champ." I said, "No, country is fine, I like it." He said, "Have you ever heard of Keith Urban?" I laughed little and said, "No I haven't. Have you guys?", talking to my team. They shook their heads no as well. Jamie said, "Its Ok, you will." Man, he was not joking. That was June 2005 and now it's June 2015 and I'm a big fan of Keith Urban, as one of his songs just came on while I'm home from Texas, and it reminded me I wanted to tell that story. Okay, hope you are enjoying my book so far.

We agreed to be involved with the promotion and do all we could to help Jamie out so he would have a successful show. We had promoted several events in our hometown of St. Joseph, Missouri and we had the biggest crowd when I fought two local guys who were around ten years younger, so we understood that people like to see two fighters they feel they know get into the ring with each other more than they do seeing their favorite fight a stranger. Jamie put us up in a huge condo right on the ocean and I would run every morning while we were there along the beachfront up to a certain point then turn around and run back. I mixed in the sprints along the way and was always dreaming about the fight and putting myself in every position I could think of, then finding a way to fight out of it to WIN.

I was taken to radio interviews, television interviews, and interviews by several different newspaper reporters while staying on the GOLD COAST of Australia and I was blessed that I had had a lot of experience with our local media in St. Joseph, so I was well accepted by all the different media. Of course everyone loved my accent, which they interpreted as being a very country, slow-talking, arrogant American. I wasn't sure how to take the remark either but I just went with it as I have always felt it's not arrogance but confidence. I'm a very honest person who is not afraid to tell you or anyone just exactly what I think if you ask me. Maybe that's why some don't ask my opinion... I had made up my mind that I could win. I was three years younger at 35 years old. I felt I had fought the better competition in the ring with Hasim 'The Rock' Rahman, Gold Medalist Audley Harrison, and two-time World Amateur Champion and Future World Heavyweight Champion Ruslan Chagaev along with many others, as this was my 66th Professional Fight.

I continued to run along the beach early each morning then we would be picked up for breakfast at one of the local restaurants so all the people could see us coming in as team with All American Prizefighter sweat suits, always matching, making it easy to see the arrogant Americans. Lunchtime would be at another local but different place, and I would usually want seafood. I fell in love with the Bay Bugs, a type of lobster, and ate them all the time along with a salad. I always drank bottled water and a glass or two of red wine. We would have our afternoon workout, hitting bags, jumping rope, touching up mitts, just keeping our rhythm down as I already felt I was in great shape, coming from the Salt Lake City fight just a month earlier.

We were all well aware of Big Bob being in training camp with

Iron Mike Tyson and they continued to pump that up promotionally as I did feel it had to help him in all aspects being in the ring everyday with the once baddest man on the planet. I was always a big Mike Tyson boxing fan and will always respect real fighters and Mike did it all for sure. I mean "4 Sho."

I remember at one of the TV interviews Bob again saying how he was feeling confident and really great, as he had spent so many weeks in training camp in America with Iron Mike Tyson. He said he was handling Mike and that Mike would always want to quit after only four or five rounds, never pushing himself, and did not have guys in his corner who were willing to push him either.

I must say I was impressed, as I was always a big Tyson fan, and was thinking holy shit, this guy took Tyson's Bombs and fired back on a regular basis for weeks. The Promoter of the event said when he picked us up at the airport, "You know, Big Bob is the best heavyweight fighter in Australia for the last ten years." I said, "Of course, but I did not only come here for a little payday; I'm looking at it as an opportunity to make big money after I win the WBF World Heavyweight Championship here in Australia." Jamie said, "I have to get him in front of the cameras for interviews as people will love seeing this good looking, cocky American." I said, "It's ok to call me cocky if you want because I don't feel it's possible to come overseas to fight the country's best without having confidence, and some may see it as cocky, but I see it as confidence. I've been training my whole life for this, not just the last several weeks, and yes sir, this will be my 66th professional fight. I started late in boxing so I had a lot of fights around the middle of the USA as a professional, improving each time almost like it was an opportunity for an extension to my short amateur career." I really wanted to WIN. I felt I had to WIN to move on with my boxing career in the path I had always wanted it to be.

THANK YOU GOD for giving me a healthy body, mind, fighting heart, and desire to be the best I can be in life, fighting just my favorite way to show my dreams and hunger to be a successful fighter and person in life. I was in control of my destiny. I was in control once I stepped between the ropes. I always loved that feeling—the nervousness would disappear once my entire body, mind, and soul climbed through the ropes. I LOVED THE FEELING OF CLIMBING THROUGH THE ROPES TO FIGHT—NO OTHER COMPARISON AS EVERYTHING YOU WANT, EVERYTHING YOU'VE BEEN TRAINING FOR IS RIGHT IN FRONT OF YOU AND TRYING TO PREVENT ME FROM WHAT I HAVE BEEN TRAINING TO RECEIVE!!!! LOVED FIGHTING! LED WITH SPEED FOLLOWED WITH POWER. 76 WINS AND 60 BY KNOCKOUT.

I was so happy a couple of days before the fight when all my training was over, Paul Briggs who was a great fighter and I'm very proud to say is one of my friends now after having the opportunity to meet him, his wife, and kids, took me to eat lunch one afternoon in Australia. He got to speak to me and find out a little about me, as he would be a guest commentator during my world championship fight with Mirovic. Paul spoke about me looking so much like his brother when he looked at me during dinner. I really like Paul and he will always be my friend, one of my closest friends from my 20-year professional boxing career.

BRIGGSY, COME AND SEE ME IN AMERICA SOON, CHAMP!!!
I OWE YOU A DINNER WITH MY FAMILY!!!

ROYAL PINES RESORT, SITE OF THE TITLE FIGHT OF MY LIFE

We had our large private dressing room. I felt perfect. I was warmed up, rested, and READY!!!

We entered the ring first. I played TOBY KEITH'S *AMERICAN SOLDIER*, STAYED OUT OF THE EYE OF THE TV FOR A LITTLE BIT THEN STEPPED INTO THE SPOTLIGHT, WARMING UP IN FRONT OF THE CAMERAS WHEN MY OTHER FAVORITE AT THE TIME AND STILL TO THIS DAY, MARSHALL MATHERS, AKA EMINEM'S *TILL I COLLAPSE* CAME ON, AS ALL I HAD IN MY MIND WAS WIN OR DIE TRYING. I WAS LIL KRAZY STILL...

COMMENTATORS:

Winner calls himself World Champion and will add the PABA Belt to his resume as well, as they have put their belt on the line, which was recently vacated by WBA World Heavyweight Champion 7' foot Russian, Nikolai Valuev, who Mirovic had taken the distance, making the winner of the WBF a top 15 of WBA, WBC and IBF.

He weighed in at an even 95 kilos and it is Cut, it is Buff, and it is Ripped AND it is All Business... ROB CALLOWAY HAS BEEN A GREAT AMBASSADOR... Great promotional tool for Jamie Myer.

What about the career resume of this guy? He has been a very busy boy since turning professional in Wichita, Kansas in 1992.

Rob Calloway, welcome to our shores, don't expect too much support. It will be sportsmanlike, we'll cheer if we have to, but we're going to cheer when we want to for your opponent, The Big Bear, Big Bobby Mirovic, on the road to Championship GOLD.

Here comes the Star and Stripes of the All American Prize Fighter, Great Ambassador and has been a great promotional tool for Jamie Myer.

He comes from the little town of St. Joseph in Missouri, 30 miles north of Kansas City and the claim to fame there is the Pony Express started there and Jesse James died there.

Big Bob came into the ring to ACDC's *Thunderstruck*.

This is going to be a David and Goliath Battle.

They sang national anthem for America first as I was the visitor and challenger. We—meaning myself and my cornermen—got fired up.

The Australian National Anthem was sang by a young lady who sang at one of our required promotional events we had to attend, and Jamie ask her to sing the Anthem before the fight. She happily agreed, of course. I loved their anthem and so did our little girl Riley Rae who would sing it after hearing and watching the video several times. I love our Lil Girl!

The announcer began to fire up the crowd by saying some comments I did not even say, like I was allowing my opponent to come in second, and I was the International Champion and my opponent only ranked #9. Oh well. He Pissed me off more than he did my opponent, I Guess.

THE STARE DOWN WAS ONE FOR THE AGES. IF LOOKS COULD KILL. PAUL BRIGGS SAID, "STARE DOWN TO END THEM ALL."

I always really believe I'm the real deal, meaning I came to Win and Win by Knocking Your Ass Out unless you're able to stop me from it. So I guess I wanted to let them know during our stare down as well. Whatever... it is what it is. LETS FIGHT...

ROUND ONE

I came out trying to maintain control in the center of the ring, using my jab to maintain the proper distance. I always like to let my opponent feel my power a little early as well, so although I was getting my jab established, I brought an overhand right on occasion as well as leading with a left hook followed by a quick right hand, staying out of danger early. I respected his size and knew he was more prepared than any of his previous fights with this being a World Title and him being in America, sparring with Mike Tyson for weeks. I really tried to just be fast and keep hitting him with my jab, adding up points to get a win in the first round, which I feel we did. Big Bob did get some short left hooks in the first in which I was able to feel his strength and power due to his size, and I feel one of those short left hooks are what caused my right eye to begin swelling so badly. I tried to land a few big shots myself just to let him know I had to be respected. I had gone over everything I wanted done after each round in my corner with my brother-in-law Jason Redmond as well as Steve Ward, my best friend, and I

153

have to say they both did a very good job, remaining calm, telling me if I won the round, and letting me relax and breathe before giving me a drink of water.

ROUND TWO

Already I felt much faster than my opponent and began with my jab, setting a quick pace and soon even tried the left hook lead followed by quick right hand after putting myself in the correct position, of course. I tried to hit his body as often as possible as I figured with his size, every bit of energy I would be able to take from him would be beneficial. I normally don't like to throw the lead right straight to the body, as it is an easy counter with the left hook. but I felt I was much faster and even loaded up on a couple of occasions to hit him in the stomach which Big Bob took ok. I began throwing my left uppercut followed by a straight right, which is my favorite punch and I can really crack with it on occasion, but it has to be set up and with Bob being quite a bit slower than myself, I used this punch combination often throughout the fight. I caught Big Bob with a lead left hook that caught him unexpectedly and knocked him off balance a little to let him know I was able to crack with either hand and I definitely had power, even for a small heavyweight. I got complimented for my power my entire career, even from world heavyweight champions like Hasim Rahman who said I was in the top five hardest punchers he had fought, and even the champ Shannon Briggs, who said, "Rob, you really got me with that first right hand." I just said thanks, Champs, as they were the two strongest fighters in my entire career.

I did not see what was going on in the other corner, of course, but watching the film, I felt although they knew Bob was a slow starter, they could see I knew how to handle myself and was beginning to get some respect for my power as a heavyweight, which I was not sure they had respected yet.

ROUND THREE

I could tell in round three Bob wanted to be more aggressive and began trying to walk me down and get closer, using his weight and power, but I was ready and prepared and moved and punched well. This might have been one of the most important rounds for me, as I realized after watching it later, he really wanted to take over at this point. Although I did not take over, I was able to hold my own and I

155

believe he felt my strength as when we would get caught up at times, I had my left jab out and on the side of his head. I would always press really hard so he felt my power every chance I got, which not only made him resist and use some energy, but had to work on his mind a little, feeling my strength as I felt they thought I was not going to be as strong as I knew I was.

After this round, Paul Briggs already began to state, "This is one of the best heavyweight fights we have seen in this country for a long time."

Big Bob's Trainer, Angelo, in Big Bobs Corner:

Do you want to put him away, Bob???????
You Love Your Mother?
You Love Your Daughter?

ROUND FOUR

I again began using my jab, mixing it up, double jabbing with a few power jabs on occasion as well as setting up quick right hands after lead hook or lead uppercut, and I was feeling comfortable with my pace as well as just maintaining the rhythm of the fight with lateral movement which I felt was giving him some difficulty. Paul said, "What Rob Calloway is doing here is like chipping away at a tree; he is just taking a little bit here and little bit there" which was exactly right.

46 Knock Outs. More KO's than Mirovic had fights...

I soon had him relaxed in the center of the ring and kept moving laterally, constantly punching every chance I got, each time with my left jab. Everything happened off the jab, even when I threw my lead left uppercut, I would bring it almost like a jab as I never dropped my left hand, I would just turn over my glove to lift his chin up a little so I could bring my hard right hand. This was my favorite combination for my entire career.

Just as the announcers said I rocked him for the second time in the fight, he backed straight up to the corner where I punched as hard as I could, mainly to his body as he would use the cross over defense, so I could not land another big shot while he was hurt. Big guys like Big George Foreman are able to use this defense pretty well.

I really felt Bob was trying to intimidate me the entire time like at the press conference, our stare down, and he would stare at me prior to the beginning of each round. Before the beginning of the fourth round, the Ref separated us into neutral corners to speak to the judge or time-keeper or just get something out of the ring, but Bob tried again to stare me down, SO I JUST LOOKED AT HIM AND SAID "YOU CAN'T WIN, BOB. YOU CAN'T WIN." I HAD NO IDEA THE ANNOUNCERS WERE NOTICING, BUT THEY BOTH MADE COMMENTS ABOUT IT BEFORE THE BEGINNING OF THE NEXT ROUND. FIGHT ME…

In the Corner, I remember Steve saying, "You've won every round, Robbie" and Jason saying, "You're kicking his ass every round" and "Keep his ass turning."

WE AIN'T KIN, SO WE CAN BEND…

ROUND FIVE

I kept my jab going and setting up two- and three-punch combinations such as spot jab-left uppercut-right hand as well as left hook-right hand, but I really started to sit on some of my right hands in this round as well.

Paul said, "What a great fight for this country!"

The announcer mentioned what I was doing with my right hand which was correct: I would step over to my left and throw what they were calling a semi-Bolo which was just an overhand right, giving Mirovic a different angle from my right hand which I was able to land and do a little damage with. Then things got a little more exciting…

I felt the round was even but with about 25 seconds remaining, Bob landed an overhand right with me close to his corner. My knees buckled, my hips buckled, and although he messed me up some, I was able to get my hands up and go with his follow-up punches, gaining some space and moving laterally until safe again. I was still a little messed up, as my head had not fully cleared up yet. I know many may not know what I mean so I want to tell you how I felt at times in my career when caught with a good punch that didn't knock you out but did everything but. You're out on your feet a little, I guess. I really was not out on my feet in the fifth round, but my head just got a little cloudy and I recovered quickly as I was in great shape and had been living right and doing the right things for months. I wanted to win and be a world champion for the rest of my life.

You think there's nothing in the punches of Mirovic; the face of Rob Calloway tells a different story. And we are not half way through yet...

I remember hitting Bob close to the bell ending the round and Angelo Hyder, his trainer, coming out into the ring. I just looked at him and went on to the corner. I met Angelo years later at *The Contender* finale and he is a great guy that I really have respect for. But I told Bob via Facebook years after the fight to tell Angelo he is lucky I didn't knock his ass out for running across the ring, yelling at me.

ROUND SIX

Before the beginning of this round, Paul said, "What a great fight this is turning out to be!"

PAUL was right again as I had to get back to work all over again just peppering away with my jab, adding up points and frustrating Bob and setting up for some big punches later.

I began to land some big punches that had Mirovic retreating to his corner and he invited me in but I just stayed away, peppering him with my jab and the announcers stated that it was a sign Mirovic has hurt him. They were somewhat correct as I was never really hurt that bad but I didn't see sense in doing anything he wanted to do during the fight, so I stayed at a comfortable distance until he came to me.

Mirovic stepped out and I continued to win the round with precise punches. When Mirovic dipped too low with his head down, I got a fair warning for pushing his head on down more, which had Bob slip on to the canvas and although I was warned for pushing down, I figured the warning was worth it because Bob is big guy and every little bit of energy I could make him use was good for me.

The Announcer stated, "The face of Mirovic is now heavily scarred, especially under that right eye."

I landed several more big shots including my favorite combination, the left uppercut followed by right hand, that again hurt Mirovic and sent him backpedalling to his corner.

Paul said, "Every second from here on out, that difference in weight is gonna show."

Paul also said, "This is a great testament to Bob Mirovic's chin as Rob Calloway is a big puncher. Calloway's face a bruise and bloody mess... Three cuts on the face of the All American Prize Fighter."

159

ROUND SEVEN

My corner was getting more excited: "I got you winning every round."

Rob Calloway lost round 5 but he came back and won the sixth on my unofficial scorecard. He is a True Professional.

Again, Bob landed a big right hand that had me shaking in my skin for just a second or two. I recovered very quickly and I felt I took over by the end of the round.

Paul Briggs: *Calloway's right hand is just a whistle after that left uppercut. Every time Mirovic is able to take the initiative offensively, Calloway is able to pull something out.*

I was not really hurt in round 7. The guys said those kind of shots are going to stay with Rob Calloway for the remainder of the fight. Later, I would jokingly say, "Paul said those punches are going to stay with Rob Calloway for the rest of his life," not just the rest of the fight.

Bob Mirovic is controlling the center ring but is not controlling the tempo of the fight.
Just when you think Mirovic is able to pull something out offensively, Calloway pulls something out.
The Fighters fought themselves to a standstill along the ropes, giving each other only seconds rest. Not your typical heavyweight fight.
They are leaving nothing in their corners.
THESE BOYS ARE TOUGH!

ROUND EIGHT

I caught Bob with quick little left hook that made him lose his balance a little, but every punch was beginning to count. I began to box more aggressively. Great Round! I soon caught Big Bob with a few combinations; several when he tried to cover and get close, I was able to put a 3-punch combination together. Although it did not appear to hurt him much, I feel the accumulation of the punches was beginning to add up.

The announcers said, "Calloway needs to get back to boxing." But I felt I was just beginning to box more aggressively, holding my own in middle of the ring and making Bob keep moving along the ropes, keeping his back to the ropes. I felt I had won the round convincingly as I finished with a strong combination in his corner, actually, a strong 5-punch combination in his corner, having me feel good about the round on my way back to the corner.

Commentator: *Calloway is at his best after he has lost a round.*

Other commentator: *Calloway is as strong as Big Bob. He has walked him back or punched him back several times.*

The Doctor, Ron Finlay, is coming up to the corner to take a look at Calloway's eye. This Fight is not going to go the distance.

The Doc asked me to look at him and I did. I was able to see out of both eyes, however, I knew that I was swollen, but I really could still see at that time. I said, "I'm good." The Doc said, "Fight on." I really thought he said fight off, so I jumped up and said "no, no!" my trainer listened to me and got upset as well, making me think I was correct. Anyway the ref got the correct information and calmed me down and I was able to get a quick drink before starting the ninth round. It was a very exciting drama in a world championship fight, for me, our corner, all the spectators, live and on TV. But the doc was correct and let me fight on as I really could still see fine at that time. Maybe the drama I bought on is what stopped him from putting an end to the championship fight over the next few rounds, but whatever. Thank God he did not stop the fight but instead, let us determine who was the world champion in the ring.

ROUND NINE

I came out holding center ring, boxing behind my jab.

Commentators:
You're going on an emotional rollercoaster with TWO Heavyweight Warriors that are riding it up front...

We have a one-point difference on our unofficial scorecard.

It is not going to take the Doctor much more and it is not going to take Mirovic many more of those left hand shots to Calloway's right eye for this to be CALLED...

Just when Calloway looks in trouble both physically and on the scorecards, that is when the American searches deep inside and finds just that little bit extra....

Paul stated: *Calloway's Punches don't seem to have the same effect as they once did so I would question if his Power is still there...*

Seconds later, I landed a left hook that I thought broke Bob's jaw. He said it happened earlier. I'm going with this left hook though.

I was able to once again land my combination of left uppercut followed by overhand right that backed Mirovic up into his corner and then landed a few more shots to put an exclamation point on this round for myself.

I LOVE YA, BOB! YOU'RE ONE TOUGH SOB. GOD BLESS
YOU, CHAMP!

ROUND TEN

Great Round! Championship rounds and I could feel we both wanted to win.

Commentators:
What an Absolute Fight. No room for the faint hearted in this center ring!

The best fight we have ever seen here in Queensland for the Heavyweight Championship!

163

Bob landed some shots, but I would put both gloves up into the air to show the spectators I was blocking them and they did not land. I knew Bob saw it too and I think a few got in, so I was hoping he would think they were not landing as well.

I felt I won boxing as Bob did not pressure too much and I felt I threw and landed more punches as well as controlling the fight with my jab and combinations.

Before the next round, Jason, my brother-in-law, said, "Two rounds… Two rounds and YOU'RE the Fucking New Champ!"

ROUND ELEVEN

Commentators:

What a great fight! These fighters have had to ask themselves questions I guess they have never had to ask themselves before.

Despite all the massive blows, Not One Knockdown!

Bob got his 2nd warning for pushing my head down as we were close and I guess I just had my head too low, so he laid on me trying to wear me out a little more. We began to both throw some big bombs.

The Announcer said, "Both men on the wrong side of 35 and still punching with all they got."

Paul said, "You really have to think about a boxer's safety" when asked if the doctor should stop the fight after this round, only leaving the final twelfth round to go.

The other Commentator said, "It would almost be an injustice to stop the fight now."

Paul: "You really have to think about the fighters safety still."

THE DOCTOR CAME TO LOOK ONE LAST TIME. I SAID, "YES SIR, I'M FINE" AND HE STEPPED OFF THE CORNER

STEPS.

LAST ROUND... I TOLD MYSELF, I WILL WIN OR DIE TRYING, AND I'M WINNING THIS FIGHT!

WHAT A NIGHT! WHAT A FIGHT!

TWO UNSTOPPABLE RHINO'S! THEY ARE ASKING QUESTIONS OF THEMSELVES THEIR BODIES DON'T HAVE ANSWERS FOR.

ROUND TWELVE

Commentators:
WHAT A GUTSY PERFORMANCE BY ROB CALLOWAY AND AN EQUALLY GUTSY PERFORMANCE BY MIROVIC!

This round was the only one I could remember not being able to see, but I didn't care. I had to win.

Commentators:
Bob needs to put in a big performance here in the last round. I don't think he has won the fight but it's admirable what he has done.

Our hearts are saying go Bob but our heads are saying we think Rob...

My right eye was completely closed and the left was closing and closing fast.

Bob has not been able to take advantage of the eye of Rob Calloway and Calloway is just an absolute warrior.

I was aggressive the last round, throwing 20 punches the last 30 seconds, being the aggressor all around the ring to Bob throwing zero. I wanted the world championship for myself, for my life of boxing, for my wife who has sacrificed more than anyone knows, for my children, for my father-in-law.

Wherever you are around Australia, pay some respect to these two....

An incredible fight!

Paul: *What a great fight, what a great fight!*

The crowd stands as one. Australia has two new heroes. Their names are Rob Calloway and Bob Mirovic.

It was a fight you only get to see very rarely. Tomorrow they will wake up battered and bruised. They will wake up tomorrow morning feeling sick feeling sore. For one of them it will all be worth it.

I haven't seen two heavyweights go at it like that in years.

Boxing doesn't always have its fans; in fact to be honest, there are plenty of detractors. What you have just seen is safe, it was controlled, and it was human emotion at its finest.

Two winners Calloway and Mirovic!

Judges:
We have a unanimous points decision:

Chris Anderson: 116-112
Danny Enright: 116-112
En Unitis has scored it: 115-113

THE WBF WORLD HEAVYWEIGHT CHAMPION IS ROB CALLOWAY!

MY 2ND TRAINER AND BEST FRIEND, STEVE WARD, PICKED ME UP FROM BEHIND. I HUGGED MY BROTHER-IN-LAW AND THEN WENT STRAIGHT TO THE CORNER AND THANKED GOD!!!

JOE BUGNER, WHO WAS FORMER WBF WORLD CHAMPION, GAVE ME MY BELT. AWESOME! HE SAID, "ROB CALLOWAY, THAT WAS ONE HARD-EARNED WORLD CHAMPIONSHIP BELT FOR YOURSELF TONIGHT!"

"I JUST WANT TO SAY, I LOVE YOU, ROBIN, CHASE AND RILEY BACK HOME. ST JOSEPH, MISSOURI, I'M PUTTING YOU GUYS ON THE GLOBE. I LOVE MY CITY, I LOVE MY FAMILY!

Commentator: *Rob, how much pain are you in right now?*

"I'M NOT IN REALLY NO PAIN RIGHT NOW... I'M TOO EXCITED!"

THE MAIN EVENT... IF YOU'VE SEEN IT LIVE BRING YOUR FRIEND, BRING YOUR FAMILY.. TELL THEM WHEN THE REPLAY IS ON.

IF YOU'RE A BOXING FAN, A SPORTS FAN, OR A FAN OF HUMAN EMOTION, YOU'VE GOT TO GET A LITTLE BIT OF THIS...

ROB CALLOWAY BEATING BIG BOB MIROVIC ON UNANIMOUS POINTS.

FOR THE WBF HEAVYWEIGHT WORLD CHAMPIONSHIP...

IT IS UNDENIABLY THE FIGHT OF THE YEAR!

I didn't look like the winner the next day by looking at the picture, but what nobody knows is Bob spent the next several weeks sucking through a straw as I broke his jaw. Well, what a fight! I've mentioned one of great things about Facebook is getting to speak to so many old friends and family members I hadn't seen in years, and Fighters, especially the ones I shared the ring with, that will always allow us to have a special bond when we put on a fight like we did June 24th, 2005 on the GOLD COAST of Australia. I hope you're doing well, Big Bob Mirovic, and GOD Bless You, Champ!

AFTER FIGHT PARTY... ROOM... ICE...

Well, after weeks of promotion and the fight living up to all the billing, there was one after party after another. However, JASON, STEVE, AND DARWIN propped me up in the hotel room with a case of water. I almost drank all of them first then of course had a couple of drinks to celebrate alone. While I spoke to my wife on the phone—yes, the hotel phone line to landline in St. Joseph Missouri, we Spoke Hours until I finally passed out—my cornermen got home sometime before we all went to eat breakfast around 11am the next morning. We had another week on the Gold Coast with parties to attend and a few other invitations from the sponsors after winning the World Championship and them finding out I was still on Gold Coast until the following week.

Everyone was as nice and courteous as you can expect. I looked like hell with my swollen eye but felt wonderful. So wonderful that at the age of 35, I and the whole team went and got tattoos. I really have always loved mine and glad I got it in Australia, as I never want to forget this feeling of winning a world championship in the heavyweight division in another country against the best fighter that country has had in the last ten years, Big Bob Mirovic... Fox Sports *2005*

Fight of the Year… Must See.

MY LOVELY WIFE ROBIN RAE HAD KC CHIEFS FAN BUS
WAITING FOR ME AT THE AIRPORT WITH ALL MY FAMILY
AND FRIENDS FROM TEAM CALLOWAY.

ALL AMERICAN PRIZEFIGHTER ROB CALLOWAY
WORLD CHAMPION

ROUND
10

One of the many great boxing friends I've met happen to be twin brothers Terry and Lee Resnick from Philly, who have been boxing fans their whole life. After getting to know me a little and seeing the fight in Australia, they said, "Rob, we need to introduce you to Marshall Kauffman in Philadelphia as he is a great trainer and with your talent, he would love to meet you. We think you guys can still accomplish a lot even though it's late in your career."

Marshall flew in and we got to know each other a little as we watched the fight from Australia and he got to meet my family and see Team Calloway Family Health and Fitness Club and the city of St. Joseph Missouri.

I remember Marshall holding the punch mitts a little and I could tell he knew I could punch. Marshall likes fighters who can punch and I feel my style fit into his training plan perfectly.

I Love Marshall and his wife Bobbie and their son Corey!!!

Great Trainer! I was able to learn so much from Marshall after the age of 35. I'm glad Terry and Lee thought of me and brought us together so I had the chance to excel to the level I thought I could get to even though it was late in my boxing career. Marshall and I will always have some great memories.

FIGHT #67
10-1-05 Roretana Tutaki, St. Joseph, Missouri W KO 2
PABA Heavyweight Championship Defense

I already had several fights set up such as bringing Tutaki in from New Zealand to defend my title I won in Australia, as he had been on the undercard and scored a big upset. I think my brother-in-law Jason was already thinking it would be a great title defense back home possibly. We went ahead with the title defense and although I remember Tutaki being a strong guy he was too easy to hit, and I soon put my right hand after several jabs, sending him to the canvas. Tutaki had a young man in his corner, Chauncy Welliver, who had been to New Zealand many times to fight and became friends with him. They even sparred each other to prepare for me. I didn't know I would one day fight Chauncy in China, of all places, at the end of my career.

Both are good guys and I'm glad Tutaki got to see the middle of the USA—GOD'S COUNTRY—St. Joseph, Missouri.

FIGHT #68
1-7-06 Ruslan Chagaev, Zenith-Die Kulturhalle, Munich, Bavaria, Germany L TKO 2

I was supposed to fight another great Russian fighter in Germany, who was 6'6 and I knew it would be a very tough fight, but after arriving in Germany, I was taken to the promoter, Hedi, who told me my opponent had a broken arm and could not fight. But Hedi said he would like to make the fight between Ruslan Chagaev and me again for our rematch from Showtime draw. After it was all said and done, I said YES. It was long way from a million dollar payday or even the $500,000 I was asking for, but it would be the biggest payday in my long great career. I have a lot of respect for Chagaev and few years later, he was very nice on TV, commenting on my toughness and picked me to win a big fight also on TV. I was happy for Ruslan that after our fight, in his next bout he was able to win the World Heavyweight Championship versus a 7' tall Russian in a 12-round war, earning a great life for himself, wife, and family. GOD bless you, Champ. You were the second hardest puncher I ever fought in my life only behind Hasim 'Rock' Rahman. I believe you were the better boxer, however. With your 2X Amateur World Championships to go along with your World Professional Heavyweight Championship and from that southpaw stance, it would be very hard to argue that.

FIGHT #69
3-18-06 Benito Fernandez Spartanburg, Fort Smith, Arkansas Convention Center W KO1

A friend of mine named Stacy 'GoodNight' Goodson was a boxer from Arkansas, who promoted several fights as well. He was able to get Shannon Briggs as the Main Event that night with me being the Featured Bout. I won by knockout in the first round versus Benito Fernandez who was a decent boxer, but I was feeling really good and was too strong as well as too good a boxer at the time.

I remember Shannon beating a guy from Omaha, Nebraska who I had always heard of but had never met until this night. We became friends as well as me working his corner that night. Dickie Ryan was a really good fighter around the Midwest and was able to fight some big names and make some money in his career. I remember Shannon later in the night when we were having a beer together said he heard me telling Dickie to get close and finish with his hook and Shannon got mad and to himself said, "OK, Rob, you got to be next." Well we would fight few years later, but I wasn't his next anyway.

I always liked and respected Shannon and unfortunately for me, we did fight few years later. I actually called up Rock who was being managed by the same guys who were really just money men helping them out until they got their payday and then taking most all the money from the fight, leaving Champs realizing or at least making me realize that thank GOD I have my college education to continue to provide for my family as money just doesn't last.

4-26-06 Jameel McCline, Buffalo Run Casino, Miami, Oklahoma
L UD 10

I called Marshall Kauffman and told him I just got a call to fight Jameel McCline in a Main Event on ESPN and wanted to know what he though. He said, "Yes, take the fight, but I need you to come to Philly to get some good sparring so we can really be prepared." I said, "Marshall, I can't as the fight is April 26th, only a couple weeks away." He said, "The money is good for an ESPN Main Event as his people must be pitching in as well to make it happen for the exposure. Go ahead and take it and I'll fly in and we can get some good gym work in anyway." So I fought top 10 Heavyweight Jameel 'Big Time' McCline with no sparring beforehand. Marshall wanted me to fight Jameel on his chest as much as possible. I said, "Seriously, Marshall?" as I've never fought like that but have always been a boxer-puncher moving around the ring etc. He said, "You have to believe you can do it first and I think you can." My local cornermen said that's crazy as he is huge and you need to box. I believed in Marshall and I'm glad I followed his plan. Actually however, I said let me come out and box the first couple of rounds and then after I'm comfortable, I will get on his chest and make it a fight. Well, Marshall taught me great lesson very soon in this fight as Jameel knocked me down in the 2nd round. It was a punch behind the head but it still was a strong punch, and I could feel the difference in strength as Jameel 'Big Time' McCline fought Klitschko in his next bout for the world title. I got up from the knockdown and was not in any trouble but got close as I could until bell rang. When I went to the corner, Marshall said, "Ok, let's get on his chest the rest of the fight and finish with your hook." I lost a 10-round decision to Jameel and one of the judges had it a one point fight and the other two had it very close as well even after the knockdown. Jameel was a great guy who said, "Rob, that was a hell of a fight" when he came to my corner after the decision. Marshall told him, "We did not have one day of sparring for this fight either!" Jameel said,

"WOW! You're kidding. Great fight, Rob!!!"

Little Story: at the Weigh-Ins for the ESPN fight, we had to do a Face-Off and then as instructed by the producer of fight, turn to the camera and cross our arms. I did. Jameel just kept staring at me. I liked it, as it was pretty cool. He was trying to intimidate me. Instead of being intimidated, I put my fist up next to his chin while I was turned for the cameras to get a good shot. OH WELL, GREAT MEMORY!!!

SOME OF MY BEST FRIENDS, AS THEY WOULD COME TO ALL MY FIGHTS, WERE ALAN WILLIAMS, FORMER RUNNING BACK FOR GEORGIA AS WELL AS THE DETROIT LIONS AND JASON SUTHERLAND, WHO WAS GREAT MISSOURI GUARD IN BASKETBALL. THEY WERE BOTH GREAT GUYS WHO WERE NICE ENOUGH TO COME AND GET ME FIRED UP IN THE LOCKER ROOM AND EVEN CARRY ONE OF MY BELTS TO THE RING. GREAT GUYS WHO WERE GREAT ATHLETES AS WELL AND I REALLY APPRECIATE THEIR FRIENDSHIP OVER THE YEARS AND I HOPE THEY MADE SOME MEMORIES THEY WILL NEVER FORGET AS I WILL NEVER FORGET THEM. THESE GUYS STARTED CHANTING IN MY LOCKER ROOM WHICH WAS RIGHT NEXT TO JAMEEL'S SO I KNOW HE HEARD IT AND BEGAN TO KNOW, IF HE DID NOT ALREADY, THAT THIS IS MY TURF EVEN IF THE FIGHT WAS IN OKLAHOMA ON TV. GREAT TIMES. JAMEEL WAS A REAL CHAMP AND I HOPE HE'S DOING WELL.

FIGHT #71
7-21-06 David Robinson, Oklahoma City, OK W KO 3

I had a friend at the fight between McCline and me, who I respected from his long career, Buck 'Tombstone' Smith. Buck was an experienced guy in the sport of boxing, to say the least, and even promoted several shows in his hometown of Oklahoma City. He asked us if we would be interested in fighting outdoors in Oklahoma City right downtown in a nice area of the city with restaurants and bars all around and we said absolutely. The venue was right next to TOBY KEITH's Bar and Grill.

Rob and Toby Keith

Robinson was another Midwest fighter who had a lot of bouts but was not on my level. I boxed aggressively and was able to stop him in the third round. Great night.

This was the last fight before my hometown fight against Byron Polley, a guy who had been talking shit for a couple years, never to my face but to the local media, including television and newspapers who went out of their way to print all they could, including having a section where anyone could call and leave comments without their name that was then printed in the Sunday Paper. I guess it became a constant for at least a year and the local reporters got caught up in the feud as well. One reporter told me, "Polley or his family members or friends would call and say we are not giving them as much coverage as we do you, and he is a professional boxer as well and its not fair." Well, they had a right to say whatever they wanted, I guess, and I had to understand people can say what they want and people love to see others FAIL. I THINK IT MAKES THEM FEEL BETTER ABOUT THEMSELVES. I *was* getting most of the attention, but I said, "I have earned it and I have won fights in Las Vegas, won fights on ESPN, won fights in other guys' hometowns who were good fighters, AND EVEN OUT OF THE COUNTRY and until these guys do that, they do not deserve any attention or at least not on the same level. Our fight was in October of 06. I had won a world title in another country and this all started close to that time. My son was only 9 years old and we read the paper daily and I was in there most of the time. I loved the attention they gave me and it would be unfair for me to say I was not happy about the bad press as I got so much great press as well. I was just saying the other fighters did not deserve to be put on an equal playing field. Anyway, one day my son read the paper before me and saw there were more comments in the call-in section. Seeing him upset made me furious, to say the least. I almost went straight to their gym and beat Polley's ass right on the street, but thank GOD my beautiful wife Robin said, "NO, ROBBIE. PLEASE."

The fight was soon made anyway with my promotional company All American Promotions agreeing to pay Byron 'The Bear' Polley $20,000 to fight me at the St. Joseph Civic Arena. He wanted one year to prepare. Sounds crazy, but this is exactly what he wanted and got. In addition to the money, he wanted all the attention right up until I KNOCKED HIS ASS OUT RIGHT IN FRONT OF MY WIFE AND SON AND ALL THE PEOPLE THAT BOUGHT EVERY TICKET INCLUDING STANDING ROOM ONLY.

I THINK SOMETIMES ABOUT MY FATHER-IN-LAW SAYING WHY DO YOU PUMP HIM UP SO MUCH AS HE USED TO TRAIN UNDER ME AS A TEENAGER. BIG DADDY SAID ONE OF THESE DAYS HE WILL THINK HE CAN BEAT YOU IF YOU KEEP IT UP. BELIEVE ME. WELL, BIG DADDY WAS RIGHT

AGAIN, OF COURSE, BUT I WOULD GET MYSELF IN GREAT SHAPE AT 37 YEARS OLD AND EVEN SAID TO THE MEDIA AND EVERYONE AT THE PRESS CONFERENCE THAT IF HE GOES THE DISTANCE WITH ME, EVEN IF I WIN EVERY ROUND, IF HE IS ABLE TO SURVIVE THE BEATING I'M GOING TO GIVE HIM, THEN I WILL RETIRE AND MOVE AWAY FROM ST JOSEPH FOREVER.

ROUND
11

FIGHT #72
10-27-06 Byron Polley, St. Joseph, Missouri W KO 2 WBE World Heavyweight Title

I told Marshall, "I have been promoting this fight for years so I do not want to pay you a 10% training deal for this fight, but I will pay you fair compensation for the bout and fly you and Travis in so you guys can be with me." Marshal said, "Absolutely" and was great. Neither he nor Travis could believe the size of the crowd to see Byron Polley and me fight. I had know idea one day I would be posting the press conference of me throwing the water bottle at him for just answering a question, but the way he did it just PISSED me off and I was at the podium and had taken my water bottle with me during my turn to answer questions from media. I guess they asked him a question, which is more than fair, and they should have, but I just didn't like the way he answered the question or the tone he used. So I guess you can say I had a lot of anger built up.

Byron went into the ring first, of course, and I remember hearing the chanting: *Byron Polley*. All the excitement, but I HEARD, FOR THE FIRST TIME, MY OPPONENT GETTING SO MUCH AP-PLAUSE IN WHAT I WAS CALLING MY HOMETOWN ON FIGHTS IN OTHER COUNTRIES AND FIGHTS ON TELEVISION FOR YEARS NOW. THIS WAS THE FIRST TIME I BEGAN TO GET PISSED AT THE LOCAL FANS AND I HAD NO RIGHT TO AS HE WAS BORN AND RAISED HERE AND WENT TO SCHOOL HERE AND ALL HIS FAMILY WAS HERE, SO WHY WAS I SO MAD? I HAVE TO BE HONEST, I DIDN'T REALIZE SO MANY PEOPLE REALLY THOUGHT HE HAD A CHANCE TO BEAT ME AND I FEEL THEY DIDN'T BELIEVE I WAS AS GOOD AS I WAS. I WANTED TO WIN FOR MYSELF BECAUSE I'M A REAL FIGHTER AND LIKE TO FIGHT AND WANT TO FIGHT. I'M MAD RIGHT NOW WRITING THIS AND I'D LOVE TO FIGHT NOW. OK... BREATHE...

THIS FIGHT REALLY DID GET ME EMOTIONAL, THOUGH. I TOLD MYSELF I COULDN'T LOSE THIS FIGHT OR EVEN LET IT BE CLOSE!!! NOT FOR MYSELF, AS I WOULD PROBABLY REALLY GO CRAZY, BUT MORE IMPORTANTLY FOR MY WIFE WHO I LOVE SO MUCH AND HAD ALWAYS BEEN THERE FOR ME AND FOR ME TO LET SOME LOCAL GUY WHO WAS BEHIND ALL THE MEDIA BULLSHIT THAT DROVE ME CRAZY FOR OVER A YEAR, ESPECIALLY WHEN MY SON READ IT, IF THIS FIGHT HAD OF BEEN CLOSE, I WOULD HAVE HAD TO MOVE OUT OF THAT CITY AS SOON AS I COULD AS I WOULD NOT BE ABLE TO GO TO THE STORE OR GET GAS OR TAKE MY WIFE AND KIDS OUT TO EAT ANYWHERE. I REALLY WOULD HAVE GONE CRAZY.

I remember helping coach my son's bantam league football team, which was one of the greatest times of my life as our daughter got to be a little cheerleader. I, of course, had dreams of him being the next Eric Dickerson... ... as he was such a great running back and ran up tall, of course, lowing his shoulder before contact, but just had a great tall running formation and I truly believed he was better on defense as a linebacker always involved in the tackles and such a smart young man on both offense and defense, knowing so much more than I did in high school. I have love and respect for all those kids who were his teammates as well as their dads who were coaches. What a great time of my life—Chase third to eighth grade during football season—I remember him taking four kids from his team with him to watch the Kansas City Chiefs play football at Arrowhead Stadium for one of his birthdays—I guess his tenth. It was around the time I was most popular in my boxing career and had many of the KC Chiefs football players who were my friends and came to my house. I was able to get great seats from a friend of mine who knew more of the guys than I did and was always introducing me to the champs and it seemed he knew everyone! 'D-Spice,' I hope you're well. Love ya, Brother. I remember taking him and Big Ed to Baltimore when I fought Rock and those TWO were eating Kentucky Derby Pies all night. Funny as it was all comped by the promoter, but he said, "Who in the Hell is eating so much so late at night, Rob?"

I took my son to the fight, of course, as I wanted him to see his daddy was not a liar and not a fake wanna-be like I felt Polley was. I'm not saying he is not the second best fighter to come out of St. Joseph, Missouri. I'm just saying he is a long way from my skill, offense, defense, boxing, in-close fighting, FIGHTING PERIOD. SO I HAD TO SHOW EVERYONE SHAME ON THEM FOR BELIEVING ALL THE BULLSHIT. I HAD MY BABY STAY AT HER GIRL FRIEND'S, WHICH IS WHAT I ALWAYS DID AS I JUST DID NOT WANT HER TO SEE HER DADDY MAD AND/OR CRAZY. POOR ROBIN RAE CALLOWAY AND CHASE— ANYBODY TOLD YOU THEY LOVE YOU TODAY? I DO!!!

I WAS SO MAD JUST WALKING TO THE RING, AND THEN SOME GIRL RAN UP CLOSE TO ME AND YELLED SOMETHING. I DON'T KNOW WHO IT WAS, BUT THANK GOD NOBODY TOUCHED ME BECAUSE I WAS REALLY A CRAZY GUY AT THAT TIME. I RESPECT PEOPLE WANTING TO SEE A

GOOD FIGHT, BUT I HAD BEEN TELLING EVERYONE WHAT SEEMED LIKE FOR YEARS THAT I WAS GOING TO KNOCK HIM OUT FAST BECAUSE HE WAS NOT EVEN GOOD ENOUGH TO TAKE A BEATING FROM ME. ANGRY STARE DOWN. PISSED.

The 1st round went just like I thought only quicker than I thought. I landed a right hand that knocked him down but he got up as it was not a big punch and I yelled and waved down at him to get his ass up as that was not even a big punch. The ref, who was a great guy and knew us both well, yelled at me to get in the corner. I did and pointed. "I'm close now!" anyway time was ticking away and then I heard the 10-second warning so I just started showing off a little like dropping my hands and then winding up my right before I threw it and it landed solid. Then again. But close to end of the round, we were against each other on the ropes and it can't be seen on video, but I know Polley remembers having his chin on my forearm at the end of the round just before the bell and I pulled his head down, choking him for a few seconds. The ref didn't notice and he knew all that shit I put up with for years was coming to an end and the truth was getting close. I went to my corner and I don't remember anything except telling Marshall I was going to knock him out this round. "He will not go past this second round."

I landed good jabs, setting everything up and then brought my right hand and then again and then the last one was so easily set up as he was in the perfect position, so I just loaded up and although it was fast punch and not my hardest. At that time, forgive me, but I wanted to knock his brains out.

Sorry to everyone who is sad to hear me say that, but after reading this far in my story, seeing how hard I worked to get where I was at and then have someone try to reach my level without putting in the work, thinking he can skip the steps, the obstacles, the hard work, the trials and tribulations I went through for years my whole life to be a successful, hardworking, honest man who loves his wife and kids and says it often, daring someone to say I don't or I haven't showed them by doing all the things a real father does, like now working in Texas so they can live in the house I built for them from a fight on Showtime, getting my head hit so hard I could not think or barely keep my balance as I said I can fight on when asked by the ref until the doctor stopped it due to the head butt. I have been through hell and this guy wants to lie to everyone, his family, friends, neighbors and to himself that he deserves to be in the ring with me, fighting for the title and more money than he has ever made in his boxing career and then have so many believe him. I'm mad because it bothered me so much. Now I understand what bothered me is the chance what he was saying was being heard and recorded for years on film on video. My son and my daughter who I would not let come to the fight would have to hear people say they watched their daddy lose to a local guy and the thought of it never being forgotten.

I HAVE TO SAY I LIKE BYRON POLLEY NOW AND HE IS A TOUGH GUY AND I WISH THE BEST FOR HIM AND HIS FAMILY AND I'M GLAD HE GOT 20 GRAND BACK IN 2006 FOR A FIGHT THAT WILL NEVER BE FORGOTTEN IN ST JOSEPH MISSOURI. GOOD LUCK TO YOU AND YOURS IN LIFE!!!

FIGHT #73
12-7-06 Doug Kaluza, Municipal Auditorium, Kansas City, Missouri W KO 2

I remember this fight some as I remember Doug being a good guy who was tough and although knocked down a couple times, kept getting up, giving it his all until knocked him out along the ropes. This was on television and my good friend BJ Flores was one of the commentators and did a great job as usual.

Doug came up to me in the lobby after the fight as I was with my wife and told me I was very good and he was honored to share the ring with me and I really thought a lot of him for saying that and I hope he is doing well in life. Doug, you're a Good Fighter and a very tough man. GOD Bless You and Yours.

FIGHT #74
02-24-07 Buck Smith, St. Joseph, Missouri W KO 3

I was a boxing fan and loved to watch fights live and so did my father-in-law. We would go anytime there was a fight within 100 miles. He took me and his friend Herb Moore. Herb would be the one who was actually driving as Herb was always a late-nighter. I loved Herb too as he and Big Daddy were really from the Old School. Anyway we saw Buck 'Tombstone' Smith put on some great fights for years. Many were set-up fights, meaning the guys really knew how to put on a show, each going down several times and Buck winning. As he was the better fighter, it was agreed upon that he would win after putting on a show for the fans. I always liked Buck and he was nice enough to put me on as a main event in Oklahoma City and always treated us well. I paid Buck what he asked for the fight with me in St. Joseph because I knew he was a real professional who would come to fight and we didn't do any of the old school stuff like entertaining the crowd by going down from fake shots or so on. But I did catch Buck with a few that knocked him down and he did get up, entertaining the crowd until I caught him with a KO punch. Great Guy and will always be a FRIEND FOR LIFE.

BUCK 'TOMBSTONE' SMITH—OVER 200 fights—RECORD.

FIGHT #75
03-29-07 Tyrone Roberts, Harrah's Casino, Kansas City, Missouri
W KO 3

I was feeling really good in the boxing game at this time. I was always athletic and loved to fight. I felt like I would control Tyrone with my Left Jab as he was orthodox, shorter, and came forward, which was a great opponent for me to box and use speed and left jab until able to drop my right hand on him. I was able to do that in the third round, getting another clean knockout.

FIGHT #76
4-18-07 Stacy 'Goodnight' Goodson, Clifford Park, Nassau, New
Providence, Bahamas W KO 2

I had agreed to fight for Joe Kelly for several fights and he and his mother were always nice to me and treated me fair. My greatest memory of almost all of my fights was when they asked me to fight on the card in the Bahamas as Joe and his family went to the Bahamas often and they always wanted him to promote a fight right there on the Beach, which was exactly what he did. I absolutely loved having my wife and kids with me for this fun, exciting, wonderful trip that my family and I will never forget. Our kids still talk about the water slides and sharks they could see through the glass and of course, my baby Riley Rae remembers getting her hair braided while lying on the beach by few of the island girls. It cost her daddy BIG but it was OK for Butter. I loved her braided hair—so Pretty! Looked like Bo Derek in *10* if you're old enough to remember that one.

I'm just glad this fight was able to happen as my opponent fell through the last minute and none other than Stacy 'Goodnight' Goodson stepped in to save the trip. It didn't take much convincing as it was an ESPN Show and in the Bahamas.

I remember Chris Byrd was the Main Event and he was always one of my favorite fighters. I really feel great that our kids got to meet him and his lovely wife and beautiful kids who remain friends of our kids on social media, of course. That was a great trip and around a year later, Marshall and I were in Vegas as I had taken my family there for Robin's sister Toni's wedding and I got in some valuable training with Marshall and Rock. Marshall and I drove out to Chris's house and sat around and visited for a while, as Chris's brother was there as well. I even told Chris I had been a fan of his since the amateurs and, "I know you're not known as big puncher as you have fought Heavyweight Champions for years now, but I remember you as a super middleweight in the amateurs and one of my best friends, Harold Roberts, fought you in Colorado Springs at the Nationals so I know you can crack, Chris." I sparred Harold for months before we left and he and I would go at it in the gym sometimes but neither ever got stopped, so Chris let me know quick he had a bright future even though I did not know he would be Heavyweight Champion one day!

I just remember Chris being a GOD-Fearing Man who was a great family man and he will always be one of my Favorite Fighters of All Time. I also saw a photo of himself and The Champ USS Steve Cunningham and it figures they would be friends as Both are REAL

189

CHAMPS, REAL MEN. I'M FAN OF THEM BOTH, IN CASE I DIDN'T ALREADY SAY SO.

STACY CAUGHT ME WITH A LEFT HOOK IN FIRST ROUND, I THINK, BUT IT WAS A GOOD LEFT HOOK, CHAMP. I ALWAYS TEASED HIM THAT I THOUGHT IT WAS ONE OF THOSE BAHAMIAN MOSQUITOES BUT HE REALLY DID CATCH ME WITH A LEFT HOOK. It didn't hurt, but he did catch me. BEST THING ABOUT THIS FIGHT WAS I LET MY SON CHASE 'KID DYNAMITE' WORK MY CORNER FOR THE FIGHT AND I BEAT STACY UP WITH A GREAT FAST HARD JAB THE WHOLE FIRST ROUND, SO MY SON HAD A CHANCE TO WORK HIS DADDY'S CORNER. THEN IN THE 2ND, I WAS ABLE TO GET HIM OUT OF THERE IN THE BAHAMAS.

FIGHT #77
5-10-07 Cliff "Twin Tyson" Couser, Crowne Plaza Hotel, Tulsa, OK W KO 2

I wish more people had got to see this fight as I feel I was at my best after sparring with Great Fighters like Steve Cunningham and Fast Eddie Chambers for weeks. Marshall was teaching me so many new things I had never been taught. I just know if he had been with me all along I would have won one of the Big 3 World Championship Belts. But I never complain and I'm just thankful I'm able to share my long career with my family and friends now.

I started with my left jab, of course, as Couser AKA Twin Tyson was a shorter right hander and after I was establishing it well with Double Jabs and a Few Power Jabs, I stepped close to him and soon as he punched back, I was protected and in punching distance again where I Let Them Go Big Time. On Fox Sports, I watched Couser beat the Cuban who had beaten Lennox Lewis and Riddick Bowe in the Amateurs in the Olympics as he was the Gold Medalist for Cuba, so I

190

respected Couser's power, but I believed in mine as well. I loved the fact I had just began to quit doing so much wasted movement and would just punch, cover up, catch, and then be right there ready to punch again and I did until I knocked him down three times and out in the 2nd round.

James 'Quick' Tillis was from Oklahoma and was there watching as well as at the weigh-ins and press conference. He began getting on Couser's nerves and Couser said, "Shut up, Quick!!!! I Knocked You Out." Oh well, I had beaten Quick as well but I respected him and wouldn't ever be disrespectful in front of everyone but OH Well. It was on soon and I was On Point with Jab, Right, Hooks, and Uppercuts. Had it all together and the dumb ass matchmaker never sent me tape of the fight. OH Well.

Rob with Joe Frazier after Rob's knockout win over Cliff Couser.

191

FIGHT #78
05-30-2007 Chris "Cold Steele" Thomas, Municipal Auditorium, Kansas City, Missouri W KO 3
Bout Shown on ESPN *Wednesday Night Fights*

This was another chance I had to fight on ESPN against Chris "Cold Steele" Thomas, who was a good fighter that I had seen fight my good friend BJ Flores. He had even been able to score a clean knockdown of my buddy, so I knew I had to be ready and I was. I loved that new style of punching with big punches and covering up for short time while they punched back with me, and then right back on them with my big blows. Real Fighting—Philly FIGHTING. I felt so good just being in the ring with Real Champs like Steve Cunningham and Eddie Chambers and Hasim Rahman and I always left for my next fight with so much confidence as I felt I had already been in the ring with the Best so there is no way I was going to Lose. Chris and I put on a good fight but I was able to get him with some big punches continuously until I Knocked him out in the third round on National Television. After going 10 with Jameel then knocking out Couser in 2 on TV and now Thomas in 3 rounds, people were taking notice that I was really putting things together and looking for a title fight soon if we could keep it up.

Around this time, my trainer Marshall brought his wife Bobbie and their son Corey to St. Joseph, Missouri to visit us and we all got a chance to go to the JAZZ Festival put on in downtown St. Joseph, Missouri. I just remember walking with Robin Rae, holding hands as always, and Marshall and Bobby doing the same behind us and Bobbie noticing all the people who would come up to me and ask for autographs or just to shake hands and later she said, "Rob, I had no idea we were with such a celebrity" and Marshall said, "See? I told you Bobby. Wait until you see the kind of crowds this guy has at his fights here in St. Joseph, Missouri of all places."

Of Course, Robin says, "Don't tell him too much as his head is big enough." I Love You Robin Rae Redmond 'Damn Redmond'

192

FIGHT #79
08-10-2007 Terry Smith, Springfield, Missouri W UD 10
Bout Shown on ESPN Friday Night Fights

This next fight was my 79th as a Professional and my second in a row on ESPN. I had sparred with Terry Smith at training camp at BJ Flores' house and I knew Terry was tough but I thought I could beat him now with Marshall in my corner. I went to camp in Philadelphia again and Marshall said, "This time, Rob, we are going to BOX" and that is how we went into camp, training harder than ever and getting into great shape with weights, running, lots of gym time with Punch Mitts, and Sparring with the Champs in Philly again. I remember the ESPN Guru, Teddy Atlas, who always picks the fights Picked ME. Terry was a Top 10 Heavyweight in the World and I'm coming up from cruiserweight but he chose me by decision. YES, HE WAS RIGHT! HOWEVER, I SHOCKED A LOT OF PEOPLE AS I BE-CAME THE ONLY MAN TO KNOCK DOWN 'TERRIBLE' TERRY SMITH IN THE EIGHTH ROUND AS HE WAS BRING-ING HIS RIGHT HAND BUT LEFT IT HANGING OUT THERE TOO LONG AND I COUNTERED WITH MY RIGHT, WHICH WAS JUST AS HARD, AS I ALWAYS BELIEVED IN MY POWER AND SO DID MARSHALL. I HAVE TO GIVE TERRY CREDIT, HOWEVER, AS IT WAS AT THE END OF THE ROUND AND HE RECOVERED IN THE NINTH AND REALLY BROUGHT IT IN THE TENTH. BUT I HAD CLEARLY WON THE FIGHT AND WAS ABLE TO CHALK THIS UP AS THE BEST FIGHT OF MY CAREER, HOWEVER, I CHOSE THE WORLD TITLE FIGHT IN AUSTRALIA AS MY FAVORITE AS I REALLY LEARNED SO MUCH MORE AFTER BEING WITH MARSHALL. I UNDER-STOOD AND REALIZED MY HEART AND WILLINGNESS TO FIGHT THROUGH THINGS THAT COULD HAVE AND WOULD

HAVE AFFECTED MANY FIGHTERS AND NOT ALLOWED THEM TO EVEN GET THROUGH THE FIGHT. BUT I WAS ABLE TO NOT ONLY WIN BUT WIN BIG AND AGAIN, OF COURSE, IN THIS ESPN *MAIN EVENT* VERSUS A TOP TEN HEAVY-WEIGHT. GREAT TIME OF MY CAREER. GREAT!!!

I must say a big Thank You to one of my favorite fighters, Steve 'USS' Cunningham, as he sparred with me or should I say allowed me to spar with him prior to the bout, which was really a huge confidence builder for me and I also got several great rounds in with another Real Philly Fighter 'Fast' Eddie Chambers who is also a great guy. I really just loved the opportunity to get to spar with World Champions like these two from Philly that always had me ready to fight anyone in the world at that time. Great memories with Marshall taking me to another level late in my boxing career, as I met Marshall at the age of 35. Marshall, we would have Ruled the World if I had met you At 25 years old. He really did bring out the best in me. I believe some trainers are made for certain fighters, meaning their training style may not work for some fighters. I really want to take my son to train with Marshall if even for just a few weeks, as I know he will learn A LOT even if they are together only once. Chase and I are different people, different fighters. I will always say he is better than me!!! My hero—'Kid Dynamite!'

One of my Favorite Stories:

I saw the Champ Teddy Atlas after a fight shortly after this one in Kansas City and I told Teddy, "I have always been a fan and I really appreciate all the kind words you said about me during my fight on ESPN." THEN Teddy said, "Hey, Rob, HOW'S CHASE?" THAT REALLY MADE ME FEEL GOOD, AS CHASE HAS BEEN A BOXING FAN SINCE HE WAS LITTLE AND IT MEANT SO MUCH FOR HIM TO GET TO MEET TEDDY AND THE OTHER ANNOUNCER. WHEN I FOUGHT IN THE BAHAMAS, I TOOK MY FAMILY AND THE GUYS LOVED CHASE AS HE WAS ALWAYS GOING DOWN THE HUGE SLIDES AND THE GUYS

WERE EITHER JUST AHEAD OR RIGHT BEHIND AND CHASE LOVED SLIDING DOWN WITH TEDDY ATLAS AND THE OTHER ESPN GUYS WHO SOON BEGAN TO LIKE HIM AS WELL AFTER I HAD BRAGGED ABOUT HIS AMATEUR BOXING CAREER. ANYWAY, TEDDY SAID, "ROB, HOW'S CHASE?"

THIS WAS MONTHS AFTER OUR BAHAMAS TRIP AND I SAID, "TEDDY, THANKS FOR ASKING AND HE IS DOING GREAT. I'M LOOKING FORWARD TO TELLING HIM YOU ASKED ABOUT HIM. THANK YOU!!!"

I REMEMBER AN AUTHOR FOR *FIGHTNEWS* AND OTHER PROFESSIONAL BOXING REPORT, PICKING ME TO WIN IN A BOXING ARTICLE AND I ALSO REMEMBER TEDDY ATLAS IN HIS PRE-FIGHT COMMENTS SAYING, "I BELIEVE ROB CALLOWAY WILL WIN THIS BOUT DUE TO HIS TRAINING AND HAVING AN OPPORTUNITY TO GET QUALITY SPARRING FOR THE FIRST TIME IN HIS CAREER WITH GREAT FIGHTERS LIKE STEVE CUNNINGHAM AND FAST EDDIE CHAMBERS, SO I'M PICKING ROB CALLOWAY TO WIN HIS BIGGEST FIGHT YET." I ALREADY HAD RESPECTED TEDDY BUT I REALLY LIKED AND RESPECTED HIM FROM THIS MOMENT ON 100%. ONE OF MY GREAT MEMORIES IN BOXING WAS HIM ASKING ABOUT MY SON WHO LEFT A GOOD IMPRESSION ON HIM, BEING A GOOD TOUGH YOUNG KID JUST HAVING FUN IN THE BAHAMAS WITH DREAMS ABOUT BEING A BOXING CHAMP. BUT TO ME, CHASE CALLOWAY ALREADY WAS. I THINK TEDDY ALREADY KNEW THIS TOO!!!

THANK YOU, CHAMP TEDDY ATLAS!

FIGHT #80
10-06-2007 Galen Brown, St. Joseph, Missouri W KO 4
IBF International Cruiserweight Title, NABA Cruiserweight Title

I had just won several fights on television, including the last one, which was considered the biggest upset of 2007 in the *Main Event* on ESPN. I had the date for the next fight and $35,000 in tickets, as the promoter knew it would be a sellout just as me and Polley's fight was. They wanted the ticket deal so they could undersell my price and still make a great payday fighting right here in St. Joseph.

I really didn't know much about Galen Brown other than he was trained by the same trainer as Polley and they trained together in downtown St. Joseph, Missouri. I was told he was being flown out to Vegas to train under a trainer whom I respected, as he had flown into St. Joseph, Missouri to train Dominic 'Hurricane' Carter when we fought in my first 'Big Fight' almost ten years before. I liked him and respected him as a trainer but I did not care if he had Angelo Dundee, Emanuel Steward, and Eddie Futch all in his corner, there was NO WAY IN HELL GALEN BROWN COULD BEAT ME OR GO THE DISTANCE WITH ME. I SAID AGAIN, IF HE DOES, I WOULD MOVE AWAY FROM ST JOSEPH, MISSOURI FOREVER!

I must say I do not have a problem now as I do not fight as a professional fighter anymore, nor do I get mad very easily. Now I love helping people rehabilitate from injuries, but years ago when I was fighting for a living for 20 years, I can say at that time I HAD PROBLEM. I LOVE TO FIGHT. I GOT MAD EASILY AND ALWAYS FOUGHT MAD. BEING IN THE EYE OF THE PUBLIC SO MUCH, ESPECIALLY IN ST JOSEPH, MISSOURI HAS BEEN BAD FOR MY KIDS, AS PEOPLE HAVE SEEN ME LOSE MY TEMPER, THROWING WATER BOTTLES, YELLING AT PRESS CONFERENCES, GOING TO MY DAUGHTERS SCHOOL, GETTING MAD AT COPS. I FEEL I HAVE ALWAYS BEEN RIGHT ABOUT EVERYTHING, SO I'M NOT GOING TO APOLOGIZE FOR ANYTHING.

I SAY BAD FOR OUR KIDS, MEANING MOSTLY CHASE SAMUEL, AS HE LOVES THE SPORT OF BOXING JUST AS I DO, BUT HE LOOKS AT IT AS A SPORT AND SWEET SCIENCE THE WAY YOU SHOULD, AND I HATE THAT PEOPLE WILL JUDGE HIM OR COMPARE HIM TO ME FOR HIS ENTIRE CAREER.

I'M AN EMOTIONAL PERSON AND IT BRINGS TEARS TO MY EYES NOW AS I'M WRITING AS I KNOW HOW GOOD CHASE IS AND FUNDAMENTALLY SOUND HE IS. I still believe he will go beyond what I've been able to accomplish in the sport of boxing and if he doesn't, I don't care, as I know how great of a young man he is and I'm so proud of the young man he has become. I Love MY Son Chase and I could not have asked for a better son for Robin and me, big brother to his sister, He is an Angel!!!

EVEN ONE TIME WHEN I WAS A TRAVELLING THERAPIST ONLY HOME FOR SHORT TIME, MY DAUGHTER CAME HOME LATE FROM BEING OUT WITH A COUPLE OF FRIENDS. I WAS WAITING UP AND SOON AS THEY CAME IN, I YELLED, SCARING THE HELL OUT OF ALL THREE OF THEM, LEAVING THE OTHER TWO TO RUN ON UP TO RILEY'S ROOM. SHE TOLD ME SHE WAS SORRY SHE DID NOT CALL, AS THEY ONLY DROVE ON DOWN TO GET SOMETHING TO EAT BEFORE COMING HOME. I WAS MAD AT MYSELF AND TOLD HER, "RILEY RAE, I JUST GET SCARED WHEN YOU'RE NOT HOME ON TIME. I CALLED." SHE SAID HER PHONE HAD BEEN DEAD. "SORRY, DADDY." I TOLD BUTTER, "IF SOMETHING HAPPEN TO YOU, I WOULD DIE." I STARTED CRYING (not sure if my baby had ever seen her dad cry before) AND SHE CAME AND HUGGED ME. AND WENT TO BED. MY BABY...MY GIRL...RILEY RAE...BUTTER.

I quit drinking for a couple weeks after yelling at my baby girl, then returned to travelling therapist and being alone in hotel each night. Yep drinking.

As I'm sitting here writing this, I think of the Press conference before Byron Polley's and my fight where I got mad and threw a water bottle and people got so excited about that Press conference that after the news hit the TV that night, we nearly sold out in hours.

Galen Brown's and my Press conference took place at the Ramada Inn finally, as we agreed to all the details and had everything signed and agreed upon long before it took place. For some reason, I was running late and had my whole family with me, meaning me, Robin Rae, Chase, and Riley Rae. Anyway this was 2007 so our kids were 10 and 12 years old. They sat on the front row with Robin Rae as I was asked to come to podium. I was already getting pissed as so many people were talking about how great of a fight this was going to be and so many really thought Brown was going to beat me. I was up there getting ready to speak to tell everyone that I planned to be 100% ready for fight and could fight right then as I was always in good shape and ready. As soon as I started talking, two of Brown's buddies came in late and were talking loudly enough that I could hear them. I could not keep my mouth shut so I said, "CAN YOU SEE WE HAVE A PRESS CONFERENCE GOING ON HERE? AND I'M THE ONE THEY WANT TO HEAR SPEAKING, NOT YOU 'FAT BOY'."

SEE, I CAN'T HELP IT. THAT WASN'T NECESSARY, BUT IT SHUT THEM UP AND I HOPE THEY ENJOYED THE FIGHT IN THE NEXT FEW DAYS. THAT WOULD BE ANOTHER HUGE SHOW FOR ST JOSEPH CIVIC ARENA.

I'm sure I have said in this book somewhere, that although Chase fights and loves Boxing, he is very much like his mother who has never had a fight in her life and doesn't even argue. She is so special and Chase is very much like his mom. Riley Rae is very special too and I love her more than anything in the world, but she is not scared to open her mouth just as her daddy is when really we need to just BE QUIET SOMETIMES!!!

WHEN OUR BABY WAS IN PRE-K, RILEY RAE TOLD US THE TEACHER TOLD HER TODAY, "RILEY, ZIP IT, LOCK IT, AND PUT IT IN YOUR POCKET."

WE WOULD REPEAT THAT FOR YEARS. I GUESS WE

STILL DO. I LUV U, BUTTER. RILEY RAE HAS SAID 1,000 TIMES, "DADDY, WE GET ALL THE BAD STUFF FROM YOU. CHASE'S FIGHTING AND MY HAIRY LEGS." OKAY THAT WAS WHEN SHE WAS 7 OR 8. FUNNY. I LUV U, BUTTER.

I'M NOT AN IDIOT, AS I KNOW SEVERAL OF GALEN'S FRIENDS SNUCK IN THE BACK DOOR FREE OR DIDN'T PAY FOR THEIR TICKET. BUT WHAT THEY DO NOT KNOW IS I DID NOT FIGHT THIS FIGHT FOR THE MONEY AND COULD CARE LESS IF I MADE A DOLLAR. I MADE SEVERAL 10'S OF THOUSANDS. BUT I REALLY DID NOT CARE ONE BIT AS I KNEW THE DIFFERENCE IN SKILL, HEART, PUNCHING ABILITY AS WELL AS THE ABILITY TO TAKE A PUNCH, AND I WAS GOING TO WIN AND WIN EASILY, FROM THE FIRST ROUND ON. I DON'T THINK I TOOK A STEP BACKWARDS. MARSHALL SAID, "ROB, WE ARE NOT GOING TO KNOCK HIM OUT IN THE FIRST COUPLE OF ROUNDS, AS I WANT YOU TO BOX AND STAY BEHIND YOUR JAB AND LET'S BREAK HIM DOWN COUPLE OF ROUNDS FIRST." MARSHALL KNEW I WAS NOT AS GOOD FIGHTING SOUTHPAWS. GALEN WAS ACTUALLY A RIGHT-HANDED PERSON BUT HIS TRAINER, WHO I NEVER HAD ANY RESPECT FOR AS A BOXING TRAINER, ALTHOUGH I LIKED EARL AS A PERSON, AND AS I SAID, I KNEW WHOEVER THEY BROUGHT IN TO TRAIN GALEN WAS ONLY GOING TO MAKE HIM WORSE.

LET ME EXPLAIN. I THINK HE IS A VERY TOUGH YOUNG MAN AND HAS MADE THE MOST OF HIS ABILITY AND AFTER GETTING TO KNOW GALEN BETTER, I SEE HE IS A LIKABLE PERSON AND I WILL CHEER FOR HIM TO BE SUCCESSFUL IN LIFE FOR HIS WIFE AND KIDS. I THANK HIM FOR BEING A FRIEND TO MY SON WHO HAS BECOME FRIENDS WITH GALEN AS WELL AND I APPRECIATE THAT.

WHAT I MEAN BY MAKE HIM WORSE IS I FEEL THAT THE MOST POSITIVE THING GOING FOR GALEN IS HIS AWKWARD UNORTHODOX STYLE WHEN HE FOUGHT

SOUTHPAW BUT WAS ACTUALLY RIGHT-HANDED AND WAS TOO EASY TO HIT AS HE SQUARED UP TOO MUCH AND DIDN'T HAVE MUCH POWER, IN MY OPINION. ANYWAY, THERE WERE MANY PEOPLE WHO THOUGHT HE WAS GOING TO BE THE NEW AND BEST FIGHTER IN OUR HOMETOWN AREA OF AROUND 100,000 PEOPLE. I have to say as it is what I feel, he is so bad, that makes him pretty good, as a real fighter thinks, who is this guy and how did he get a good record fighting the way he does—converted southpaw who squares up with not a lot of power and will lead with a damn uppercut out of nowhere. I have said he is so bad that it makes him good. I was in the locker room getting ready to come out for our fight and I hear the crowd chanting "Bad Boy Bad Boy" I came to the ring again with the hometown boy being Galen and I have now came to accept that just like Byron he was born there and went to school there and had wife and kids from there just as I did, but him being raised there made a difference. I will say I again had my fans, friends, family members, all sitting around the ring and in the stands and feel I actually had more people cheering for me. But his followers were mostly younger as he was 12 years younger than me, and the way they acted or I made them act, however I put it, they made sure this would be the last time many of the people would ever come to another boxing event downtown, for quite a while anyway, to say the least.

WELL, I'M GETTING ON TO THE NEXT FIGHT. THIS FIGHT WAS EASY JUST LIKE I SAID IT WOULD BE. I JABBED HIM AND WHENEVER I WANTED, I PUT MY HANDS UP AND GOT CLOSE, KNOWING HOW TO HANDLE MYSELF FROM BEING ON HIS CHEST AND ACTUALLY PREFERRED TO BE FIGHTING FROM A CLOSE DISTANCE THE OLDER I GOT. GALEN IS A TOUGH YOUNG MAN WHO IS NOT SCARED TO FIGHT ANYONE, BUT NEITHER AM I AND I HAVE A LOT MORE ATHLETIC ABILITY AND ALL AROUND BOXING SKILL. I TOLD MARSHALL AFTER THE THIRD ROUND, "I CAN NOT STAND IT ANYMORE, MARSHALL, I'M KNOCKING

HIS ASS OUT THIS ROUND" AND MARSHALL SAID, "OK, ROB, GET HIM OUT OF HERE." WATCH YOUTUBE: ALL YOU NEED TO SEE IS ROUND 4.

I HOPE I DIDN'T COME OFF TOO DISRESPECTFUL TO MANY OF MY FAMILY AND FRIENDS WHO WILL READ THIS LATER, BUT YOU DON'T UNDERSTAND THE SHIT I PUT UP WITH FROM THE ONLY TWO GUYS I FOUGHT FROM ST JOSEPH, MISSOURI EVEN THOUGH THEY WERE 10 AND 12 YEARS YOUNGER THAN MYSELF. SORRY IF I DID. LET'S MOVE ON TO THE NEXT FIGHT.

FIGHT #81
02-23-2008 Matt Gockle, St. Joseph, Missouri Fought South Paw
W KO 2

My son Chase was really doing well as an amateur boxer, winning the National Junior Golden gloves in Las Vegas as well as the Ringside World Tournament to go along with his many Silver Glove Championships so I put on a Pro-Am show at the St. Joseph Civic Arena where we could fight on the same card together.

He looked great as usual, putting his punches together like a little pro, beating his overmatched opponent who was older and heavier but did not have near the experience Chase had. It was a successful amateur show and I'm glad Chase had an opportunity to fight before my bout. I fought a young man from nearby Topeka, Kansas who had trainers and a manager who were friends of mine and I thought he could use the money, and although it wasn't a big payday, I hope it helped out a little. Gockle brought a good fight and did his best, but I was feeling really good at this time in my career and after the first round where I mainly threw my jab, Marshall told me, "Rob, go out this next round and fight southpaw the whole round and don't turn back." I smiled and said, "Okay, Coach, you got it."

I began with throwing my right jab which didn't feel to comfortable, so I began just getting closer and throwing 1,2,3, right jab, straight left hand, followed by right hook. After about 3 or 4 of these combinations, I dropped him face first from my right hook.

He was a good guy and I respected him for taking the fight and around a year later, he came up to me and said, "How are you doing, Rob?" He shook my hand and I talked, but I had my mind on my son as we were at one of his amateur bouts, so I didn't spend too much time or, I guess, any bullshitting with someone I didn't seem to know. Well, soon as Gockle walked off, my brother-in-law Jason said, "You didn't know who that was, did you?" and I said, "No. Did you?" He said, "That was Gockle who you just knocked out few months ago." I said, "Damn it, Jason, you need to talk. Tell me if know I'm not remembering who he is. I liked him, he was a tough guy."

Oh well…

FIGHT #82
03-15-2008 Juan Robles, Allentown, Pennsylvania W KO 8
WBC Continental Americas Cruiserweight Title

ESPN: EAST COAST. SHOWED ON OUR LOCAL CABLEVISION SEVERAL TIMES AS WELL.

This next bout was the first one I began to feel old or maybe I was just recovering from being very sick with the flu with a fever. I didn't train or run much as I was really sick as hell, terrible, and I was 39 years old, almost 40. My heart and balls got me through this fight. I've been told, "Rob, you were behind on all three judges' scorecards after the sixth round." Juan Carlos Robles was undefeated at the time and had some decent power. He came in good shape and tried to pressure, being aggressive, however, I was doing well holding my own, of course, and if I was indeed behind, I bet I won at least 2 or 3 of those first few rounds anyway. Oh well, it didn't matter anyway as I kept putting pressure on him behind my jab and just kept trying to land my right hand either before or after my left hook. The fight was very good, to be honest, but I had been in tough fights many times and I feel he had not, as he was UNDEFEATED at the TIME. Until my pressure kept coming and in the eighth round, he had his back to the corner and he stepped out to his right, which was correct as he did not want to get hit with my right hand again. But I loved the combination left uppercut followed by right hand, which did not work with Juan Carlos as much as the left hook followed by my overhand right, especially late in the fight, when the guy relaxes his mind a little getting lazy. He steps to his right correctly but with his right down, not ready for the left hook I threw, followed by a huge hard very angry overhand right that knocked his ass out, laying him out in the corner until the docs woke his ass up. I had some meanness, as this was for the WBC International Championship and he was undefeated and his people and many others believed he would win. I was really sick as it took everything I had to pull the fight out. I NEED TO SAY THANK YOU, MARSHALL, AS YOU COACHED ME AND PULLED OUT THE PUNCHES FROM MY SICK BODY TO KNOCK HIM INTO THE MIDDLE OF THE FOLLOWING WEEK IN OUR CORNER.

I'm sitting here writing this autobiography and I feel this was my last fight, as I would never feel the same in the ring again as a fighter. I turned 39 just a few months later and although I don't like to use age or say age caught up with me, it definitely did. My next training camp would be in phoenix, prior to the Max Alexander fight, instead of Philly as rock had a fight in Los Angeles so we had camp in phoenix. I felt horrible in that training camp. But I feel it may have started in this fight…

HOLD ON. WE CAN'T FIGHT AGE; I TRIED HARD TO…

I USED to say I don't give a damn about money, as I do not need it to be happy. My wife would say, "Robbie, don't say that as you do." I know she is right as I'm here in Texas, working for money to pay the bills and I fought all over the Damn World for money to pay the bills. I guess sometimes I feel I wish I had a little apartment like I do for myself here in Texas, only this home is where we raised our kids and just working and having money for things and not having to worry about all the other bullshit that we put ourselves through to provide the best we can for our family. I was almost 39 years old and I hadn't made enough money to retire from boxing yet. I had 82 Professional Fights, winning titles, WBF World Championship and defended it a few times before losing to Chagaev in our rematch and the biggest payday of my career. In his next fight, Ruslan Chagaev won the World Heavyweight Championship and then lost the Unified Championship Fight with Wladimir Klitschko from Ukraine and is still considered the World Heavyweight Champion, June 2015. I remember seeing him prior to one of his title defenses in Germany. He was actually on his way to the ring with his entourage and he said, "Rob Calloway" and I walked up to him and shook his hand and said, "Good Luck, Champ." Great memory and great feeling to have a Great Champion like Klitschko even know who I was. I think one of his guys walking to the ring told him who I was— I'm sure he did, as I saw him saying, "Wladimir, I think that there is Calloway."

I want to let everyone know these next few fights—next few years—were HELL. I brought it on myself. I lived a dream for years and I'm a Real Fighter. I don't need anyone to feel sorry for me; I'm not asking for a handout. I will handle my business. I'll take care of Robin Rae Calloway, Chase Samuel Calloway, and Riley Rae Calloway.

Hang On...

Well, I had Team Calloway still and I wish I had sold it this year. I wish I had taken the $80,000 payday for a WBO World Cruiserweight Championship fight in Wales on the undercard of the WBO Middleweight Champ.

Anyway, here we go...

I was told by a promoter from St. Louis who had watched me beat Terry Smith on ESPN and then beat Chris Thomas on ESPN that he would like to speak to me about signing me up.

What people do not know is I spent so much money, as I bought the biggest house I could build after fighting Chagaev on Showtime then I blew hundreds of thousands on Team Calloway, keeping it going instead of closing when people started cutting back on their money as everything was getting tight for everyone at this time. But I just didn't think, didn't care enough as I just assumed I could keep fighting for money and I was never going to get old.

I have to say my wife Robin has ALWAYS PAID OUR BILLS. I'VE NEVER WROTE A DAMN CHECK. I'M NOT HAPPY TO SAY, BUT I'VE NEVER COOKED A MEAL. HELL I USED TO NOT KNOW WHAT I WAS WEARING THAT DAY UNTIL SHE LAID IT OUT ON THE BED. YES, I'M EMBARRASSED AND I HOPE MY DAUGHTER NEVER DOES THIS AND I BET 100% SHE WILL NOT.

ROBIN PAYS ALL THE BILLS. OK, I MAKE THE MONEY OR WE DID TOGETHER AS WE BOTH OWNED AND OPERATED TEAM CALLOWAY 50/50, BUT I FOUGHT AND PAID FOR EVERYTHING AND YES, IT WAS ALL MY FAULT AS SHE DID NOT EVER ASK FOR ANYTHING. EXCEPT FOR ME TO QUIT SPENDING MONEY. HELL, AS I'M WRITING THIS, I'M THINKING SHE STILL TELLS ME THAT. I'M LEARNING, ROBIN RAE. BE PATIENT. WE HAVE ONLY BEEN TOGETHER ALMOST 30 YEARS NOW…

FIGHT #83
05-22-2008 David Robinson, St. Louis, Missouri W KO 2

I was approached and asked to sign a 3-year contract with Steve in St. Louis, as we had a mutual friend, Derrick Spicer, who introduced us and wanted us to get together, as he thought it would be a great fit. I still like Steve and his buddy the lawyer, both of which I feel are good guys who mean well, but money is always the root of all evil. They didn't give a damn about me or taking a serious chance, as I had already been approached to fight for the WBO World Championship in Wales but didn't take it, as Marshall and my wife Robin both said that it was not enough money and they could pay double what they were offering. I have regretted not accepting the offer ever since I turned it down. I will never be mad at my wife as she always thought I have deserved to make millions every fight but my trainer, Marshall Kauffman said that is not enough money and I believe he was right as I was top ten by everyone at that time and had won several fights on TV in a row at the time. But I needed money to pay the damn house payment for the house that I had to build, a 4 story "mansion" in Carriage Oaks. I'm glad we are still there and raised our kids in the house I had built in 2002 but damn it, I hate the boxing bullshit I went through the last few years of my career. The crazy feeling, getting drunk any chance I could to make me feel a little better about losing that little bit of speed that separates the top 10 from everyone else. Hell, I can still punch hard and I'm 45, but I cannot hit a top 10—hell top 30—athlete anymore with consistent punches which is what made me retire. Then again. Then again. My wife told me years before my last fight, she knew I was not the fighter or acting like the fighter I was with the drinking, not training, etc.

FIGHT #84
7-19-2008 Max Alexander, Civic Arena, St. Joseph, Missouri D 12
WBC Continental Americas cruiserweight title Defense
Shown Tape Delayed on Fox Sports Network

I still really didn't think I was losing anything until Marshall told me we were going to move camp from Philly to Phoenix as Hasim 'Rock' Rahman was going to fight a couple weeks after camp in Los Angeles versus James Toney, whom I was supposed to fight.

I was actually in camp in Philly to fight James Toney. Posters were made and then we got the call that Rock was going to be fighting

206

him for the number one spot, so we remained in camp and the new promoters made a fight to promote in St. Joseph, Missouri. They knew I had had a huge following there for years and this would be a chance to get some of their money back, as they had agreed to pay me $2,000 a month so I could concentrate on boxing only and be ready for the next fight. Of course, they knew I had not taken the $80,000 title fight in Europe and they believed I would be getting another call soon so they could get all their money back and then some. BUT they should have talked to Marshall first on my opponent or who it should be. They thought fighting The Contender fighter, Max Alexander, would be a big sale and all would be good. Well as I said, I was SHIT in training camp for the first time ever.

I had lost that little bit of speed, the speed that separates top 10 from rest. I could still punch, but getting out of the way of punches and top speed had left me. I felt it at camp and then with all the animosity from Steve toward Marshall and Marshall toward Steve, I felt terrible the whole camp. Going into the twelfth round, the fight was even on the cards, I was told, as the second in my corner was doing his job for Marshall and getting the scores. ANYWAY, MARSHALL POINTED HIS FINGER IN MY FACE AND SAID, "I TOLD YOU. I TOLD YOU. I TOLD YOU. THESE IDIOTS SHOULD HAVE CALLED ME FOR AN OPPONENT, NOT CALLED YOU!" THEN HE LEFT.

Marshall meant I did not need to be fighting a young guy who was used to sparring tough and fighting tough, being from Philly. He said I needed an older fighter or young guy who did not have the speed, etc.

I started the twelfth round after I really thought I won the first six easily. By the end of the eleventh, though, I really thought I was losing, as Max wasn't doing anything special but just landing more than I was. It goes without saying, yes, this is the fight I got old. But I had heart and I kicked his ass the twelfth round and thought that would allow me to win the decision. Hell, I was the champion and defending my international championship, not Max Alexander. He was the opponent who got his ass beat easily six rounds then I beat him the twelfth, in my opinion. Easily and, Max, you're lucky I didn't knock your ass out in the twelfth. The three judges had it me winning one, max winning one and one even. IT WAS A DAMN DRAW WITH ME BEING DEFENDING CHAMPION AND WINNING THE EARLY PART OF THE FIGHT AND FINISHING LIKE A CHAMPION BY WINNING THE TWELFTH BIG BUT IT IS WHAT IT IS, WAS WHAT IT WAS.

I've mentioned Facebook several times throughout this book, and it was good for me to understand I was respected as a fighter from many great fighters around the world and one being a great world champion and a great friend from the sport of boxing, USS Steve Cunningham. A real champ from Philadelphia.

THANKS FOR THE KIND WORDS AND LETTING ME KNOW: ONCE A CHAMP, ALWAYS A CHAMP. LITTLE SLOWER WITH HAND SPEED BUT ALWAYS A CHAMP NONETHELESS.

I always respected the comment, as Steve is exactly right. It's that little bit of speed that separates fighters from top ten and those who become world champions. I like to think I'm still fast and I am to the normal person and even boxers in the gym that are not professionals, but Steve is exactly right. Once that little bit of speed leaves you forever with age, you never get it back—speed of punches, speed of being able to slip punches, speed…

FIGHT #85
2008-09-27 Alexander Alexseev 15-0-0 Color Line Arena, Altona, Hamburg, Germany WBO Championship L TKO 3 (12)

I was still the WBA International and IBF International Champion and I was still the WBC International Champion, as I did not lose the belt with the 12-round draw in the previous fight. But everyone assumed with the fight being in my hometown of St. Joseph, Missouri, that I must have lost, so it did not take long for the phone to be ringing off the wall. I had not lost but was awarded a damn draw in my home-town, and I was worse than I had been in years. True, age snuck up on me… True.

Losing the fight in Germany to this Russian drove me crazy as I was already getting crazier and older each day in the ring and I was not even spending time in the ring as no more camps in Philly. Marshall and I were done. St. Louis guys were a joke.

More after next fight…

FIGHT #86
2008-12-06 Grigory Drozd 30-1-0 Circus, Nizhny Novgorod (Gorky), Russia L TKO 7 12 WBO Asia Pacific Cruiserweight Ti-tle. WBC Cruiserweight title. PABA Cruiserweight Title

Calloway down 8 times (1 time in rounds 1, 2, 4, 5, 6, 7; 2 times in round 3).

I DID NOT TRAIN… NO SPARRING… CRAZY AFTER EVERYONE WAS HOLDING MY NUTS UNTIL I GOT DRAW WITH MAX AND THEN LOST IN GERMANY. I TAKE THE BLAME 100% AS I DID NOT WIN. SIMPLE.

OF COURSE, I HAVE WATCHED THE FILM ONCE TO SEE WHAT THE HELL HAPPENED.

I remember this is around the time my brother-in-law stopped talking to me. I still kept him in my corner, but we are opposite people. I talk too much and Jason does not talk at all, or enough. I could go on and explain and give facts, examples, but it is what it is. We were close for many years so I don't feel I have anything to explain. It is what it is. OR was what it was. Get good at making excuses, its diffi-cult to excel at anything else…

I DRANK ON THE PLANE, WHICH WAS THE LONGEST FLIGHT OF MY LIFE. I HAD BEEN TO AUSTRALIA, GER-MANY, POLAND, SO MANY OTHERS, BUT WOW, EASTERN

RUSSIA… I REMEMBER FLYING TO GERMANY, THEN MOS-COW, THEN ANOTHER PLANE, WHICH WAS SCARY AS I STILL REMEMBER IT CIRCLING AND LANDING VERY QUICKLY.

You would think after all the flights I've been on around the world I would be used to flying, but I really was not. The most scared I had been was when Robin and I were on a flight together from Vegas, as I had taken her there without the kids one weekend. Surprisingly, I was nervous as hell, especially on the way home, thinking of the kids. I'm ok when I'm by myself, as I know our kids will be ok with their great mommy always taking care of them, but with us both on the plane together, if it goes down… I know I drove Robin crazy too.

I realized, or now I do, that I had become an old fighter (6 months from age of 40) who needed rounds to get warmed up and into the fight and this 28-year-old Russian who was a champion and very good was not going to let me get going. I was still tough and got up and brought the fight all I could, but he was too fast for me and he beat me, well, actually knocked me down several times. I said to myself on the plane to Russia, "I hate my life and I plan to win or I want to die try-ing" and I really meant it at that time, I think.

YES, I WAS DOWN EVERY ROUND ONCE EXCEPT FOR ROUND 3 WHEN I WAS DOWN TWICE. I TOLD YOU I WAS READY TO DIE. I FELT TERRIBLE AS A FIGHTER. AS A MAN. I was almost 40. Team Calloway, Our Family Health and Fitness Club was going under and I had put SO much money in it. I must take the blame for it and I will and I have. Also screw the guy at Commerce Bank who called and asked for Robin and I said, "She's not here right now but can I help?" He said, "Noooooo" in a whiney voice and said, "Just have Robin give me a call." I had just taken the fight in Russia to bring our note up to "0" but the wonderful gentleman said they were going to foreclose as we had missed payments in the past and they had just decided to foreclose on the note, as the business was too risky at this time. I'm glad I was able to give them a substantial amount of money every month for 10 years as well as free memberships, and free tickets to fights on occasion. OH WELL, MONEY IS THE ROOT OF ALL EVIL.

I was depressed, but I always feel that is easy way out, so I will not say I was a depressed, weak individual. I will explain I was 40 years old with almost 90 professional fights all over the world and although did well, never felt as though I did well enough. But thank GOD I did get a college education so even after not making the money I should have as a professional fighter for twenty years, or owning and operating a popular Family Health and Fitness Club for ten years, I could studied my ass off for a year, taking hundreds of hours of Continuing Education so I could acquire my Missouri LPTA License again to begin practicing as a therapist. I forgot not too many professionals at the hospitals were big boxing fans, but most importantly, I forgot that in the last ten years while I had been paying attention to Fightnews.com or Boxrec.com and even RobCalloway.com all before Facebook took over, that Professionals in the Medical Field had also all went to computer systems for their notes, billing, etc., leaving me, once I did return to Physical Therapy, LET'S JUST SAY LOST…

FIGHT #87
2009-11-07 Clinton Boldridge, Civic Arena, Saint Joseph, Missouri, USA W KO 5 (10)

MY FIRST "RETIREMENT FIGHT," 40 years old

We were supposed to fight a fighter from Shreveport, Louisiana, as he had beaten Galen before and we thought that would make for an easier promotion even though I did not realize we even needed to promote my LAST FIGHT. OH WELL. We did need to promote it and although it would not be against the Shreveport fighter. Even though we flew him and his manager in and gave them money for their time, they did not take the fight. I'm not going to even mention his name. I

211

actually like the guy, as I've seen him on a couple of occasions now while I've been here in Texas on the Louisiana border working in Physical Therapy.

I'll just say we fought a guy who I liked and would rather give him little money than anyone else around that time as he was around my age.

FIGHT #88
2009-12-18 Pawel Kolodziej 23-0-0 MOSiR Hall, ul. Ks. Skorupki
21, Lodz, Poland L RTD 6 12
International Boxing Cruiserweight Title

MY SECOND "RETIREMENT FIGHT," 40 years old

Steve, Rob, and Jason in Poland.

I was 40, retired, and trying to figure out what I was going to do the (hopefully) next 40 years of my life now that I knew my boxing career was over, or at least me getting better as a fighter in the ring was over anyway.

I realized I was perfect for some young future champs as an old champion who has a resume and big names on the list of my opponents so the promoters can promote their young champion to be able to say their guy did better and was able to beat Calloway sooner than the other contender did soooo, I probably made more money in next five fights than any other five fights put together.

I got a call from the promoters/managers of Briggs to see if I wanted to fight Shannon on the east coast. I said yes. I sent Rock a thank you as I had told him I was needing some money so I would appreciate a fight if his managers would hook me up. Rock didn't return my text and he always does except this time, letting me know he did not have anything to do with it and also maybe he did not like the fight for me. But as I said, with Team Calloway ready to close up, I had to sit down and decide what we were going to do. Robin and I both said, "Lets close Team Calloway and move to St. Joseph Avenue" down from Lafayette High School where Chase told us he and Riley Rae wanted to go for high school. I'm glad we got chance to have Team Calloway on the Avenue for a year or so and I'm also glad we closed after a year and I decided to only train Chase from our home gym in our 3-car garage transformed into Team Calloway for Chase to continue his boxing career as long as he wanted.

FIGHT #89
2010-05-28 Shannon Briggs 50-5-1 Scope Arena, Norfolk, Virginia, USA L TKO 1 (10)

MY THIRD "RETIREMENT FIGHT," 40 years old

Shannon was the Former Heavyweight Champion of the World and went 12 rounds for Championship next fight after ours.

Shannon's people called and wanted me to fly in for a Press Conference to announce the upcoming fight with Briggs and me. I said ok of course, but I needed 2 tickets and accommodations, as I want to bring my son Chase, who is great amateur and will enjoy the trip.

I have to say TWO THINGS about our Fight:

#1 Shannon hit me with a great body shot in the 1st round. I remember I threw my right hand and he slipped to his left correctly and believe it or not, it was like slow motion as I saw his left foot pivot out with his heel transferring his weight correctly into the punch. I'm crazy to actually remember this as I really do remember the perfect form of his punch and he really got me with the body shot to the my right side. I stayed down until the count of 8 with Shannon being in a neutral corner. I looked at him after I stood up and he just shook his head, as if to say, "Stay down, damn it, Rob" as he and I had become friends at an earlier fight in Arkansas. We spent a few hours at the bar, talking and enjoying the night. I remember Shannon telling me, "Rob, I heard you coaching Dickie in the corner and I said ok, Rob's got to be next." I said, "Dickie is good guy and although we're both from the Midwest and fought a lot of the same guys, we really did not know each other until tonight. Hell, we're friends now and he asked me to work his corner." Great Night! Good Friends: Dickie and Shannon 'The Cannon' Briggs. Good luck on your quest to regain the Heavyweight Championship! Also you owe me a visit to St. Joseph, Missouri to see my son fight.

#2 I just remember Shannon being very strong. Rock hit me the hardest ever and Chagaev next, but I remember Shannon just being very strong and I also remember he is a good man and was nice to my son Chase and I appreciate it. SHANNON HAS TOLD ME ON A FEW OCCASIONS, "ROB, YOU REALLY GOT ME WITH THAT RIGHT HAND YOU CAUGHT ME WITH. SERIOUSLY, YOU CAN PUNCH!" I just said, "Thanks Champ, and I don't have to tell you what I think of you!" Shannon was the only man in 20 years as a Professional Fighter to stop me in the first round. I got up from great body shot, but he rushed in and I really don't think he caught me with another punch, but the Ref stopped the fight, as many at that time had become familiar with me and just did not want to see me get hurt. I could have gone on, of course, but I really like Shannon and hope he gets the World Championship again.

Thanks for giving me the fight when I called and said, "Shannon, I'm trying to save my health club and home and need some money, Champ. Can We Fight?" A couple days later I got a call for the fight. I will always be a fan of Shannon 'The Cannon' Briggs and I will always appreciate you being a friend to my son, My Hero, Chase 'Kid Dynamite' Calloway. Thanks.

I had fought all over the world, was 40 years old, and the best was far behind me, and I got a call from some guys in KC who wanted to do a retirement fight for me in Kansas City, so I agreed and they got an opponent that I had previously stopped in his home state.

215

I worked Chase's corner in the Ringside World Tournament the day before the fight then we left from our hotel with Kid Dynamite's World Championship belt and travelled across town for my fourth retirement fight.

FIGHT #90
2010-08-06 Travis Fulton 14-24-0 Memorial Hall, Kansas City, Kansas, USA W 6

MY FOURTH "RETIREMENT FIGHT," 41 years old

Travis was a tough guy who had a great MMA background and went the distance most of the time. I outboxed him, I thought, pretty clearly and he did go the distance, but I later found out who the Judge sitting nearest to our corner was: a friend of Travis's from the MMA circuit and he was nice enough to call the fight a draw. Thank GOD the other two judges scored it for me easily and I won my 76th Professional Fight and retired for the fourth time in my career after my 90th Professional Fight.

On my way out of the ring, I noticed the Judge who was the MMA fighter and had voted for Fulton—or scored even, which was just as bad to me—so I told him just what I thought of his scoring and how embarrassing it must be for him to have to live with himself being a coward, trying to hurt a real fighter by hiding behind his judging table.

OH WELL, AGAIN HOW MANY TIMES HAVE WE ALL AS FIGHTERS, COACHES, FANS, BITCHED ABOUT A BAD JOB OF SCORING BY SOME JUDGE. Thing is I won, of course, and he had it a draw, making it a win by majority decision instead of unanimous decision, but OH Well. Over.

FIGHT #91
2011-10-03 Chauncy Welliver 49-5-5 People's Stadium, Tianjin, China L UD 12
WBO Asia Pacific Heavyweight Title, WBO China Zone Heavyweight Title

MY FIFTH "RETIREMENT FIGHT," 42 years old

Well, I was retired for over a year, was 42, and asked to take a fight in China of all places. I agreed as it was against Chauncy Welliver who had KO'd Byron Polley and Galen Brown, who were the only two locals I had fought. I didn't believe Chauncy could knock me out or even beat me in a 12-round title fight. See, I've learned after all the years, all the fights, you really have to feel you're going to win the fight before the bell rings. No matter what, I always thought I'd win every fight prior to the opening bell.

I remember Chauncy being in the best shape of his life, however he had always been a fighter who had a weight problem. I think his size allowed him to be one of the best sparring partners, as he was flown all over the world to be a sparring partner and with his manager, who was a wealthy business man, Chauncy had the support to get the best of everything, and sparring being the most important.

I still thought I was a professional fighter, although I had not acted like one in a while now, at least for a couple of years anyway. We flew to Beijing, China and then over to Tanjing, China for the fight. We were well taken care of and it was a great experience to see a totally different part of the world, CHINA. I remember all the people walking the streets. Picture 100,000 people walking the streets of downtown St. Joseph, Missouri and that's what it was like. Everyone was very nice and we were treated all very well. I remember going to the Arena for the Weigh-Ins and I said, "WOW, you think this place will be close to being full?" Well I remember the next night watching the fights much earlier in the day prior to our main event and soon thousands of military fully dressed in uniform marched in, taking up all the remaining nearly 20,000 seats. Wow.

Chauncy boxed right with me early on. Maybe he knew it was important to start early, as I was 42 and really felt much better after the fourth round once we got into the fight a little, but he did the right thing by forcing me to get my act together as soon as possible.

I thought the first five rounds were close, but I felt the rest of the fight would be mine as although I was 42, I always felt better the longer the fight went. Well, I remember Chauncy telling me he had been sparring with a Russian in the training camp in Russia. Oh well, I did not spar ONE Day and I was shadow boxing and hitting the heavy bag a little, but I knew I could fight and the longer the fight the better for me. This was for the WBO International Championship so it would give me a chance to get yet another big payday if I could win. I really thought I would, but I have to give Chauncy credit, as I remember thinking, *ok round five I'm going to really pick it up now and beat his ass*, but he deserves the credit as I hit him hard and often but he was able to take the punches and punch me right back just as often. CHAUNCY WAS RIGHT, WE REALLY GAVE THE CHINA CROWD ONE HELL OF A FIGHT. Well, I hope he and his wife and his manager are all well and I appreciated the opportunity late in my career to fight a Top 5 Heavyweight and International Champion at the time, which would have given me a chance to get yet another payday anyway. BUT AS MY WIFE ROBIN RAE WOULD SAY, "WHEN IS ENOUGH GOING TO BE ENOUGH? BILLS ARE ALWAYS GOING TO KEEP COMING AND YOU CAN'T FIGHT FOREVER, ROBBIE. YOU CAN'T FIGHT FOREVER, DAMN IT!" I LOST A 12 ROUND DECISION BUT FOR SOME REASON, I GUESS I THOUGHT I COULD STILL FIGHT ANOTHER.

STARTED TO LISTEN TO MY BEAUTIFUL WIFE ROBIN. WELL, AFTER MY NEXT FIGHT IN AUSTRALIA, I LISTENED...

ANYBODY TOLD YOU THEY LOVE YOU TODAY, ROBIN RAE? I DO!!!

FIGHT #92
2012-03-17 Mark de Mori 17-1-2 Entertainment Centre, Gladstone, Queensland, Australia L TKO 4 (10) WBC Asia Council Continental Heavyweight Title

MY SIXTH "RETIREMENT FIGHT," 42 years old

I remember getting a call at Team Calloway from a boxer asking for an opportunity to come and spar as they knew I beat Mirovic and would like to come and spar. I wasn't sure if it was a joke or what, but I said I'm in St. Joseph, Missouri just north of KC, but we're not paying to bring anyone over from Australia to America to spar. He said,

"Ok, thanks" and hung up. All good. I actually like the guy, Mark, now. He is a good guy and I like him, but I must say, I feel the fight was stopped too soon as I was coming on and feeling good when the ref stopped it, but whatever. I was a slow starter at this time in my career to say the least, as it took four or five rounds just to get my body warmed up and into the fight. The locker room was hot enough to warm me up, I guess they believed, however, Mark caught me with a big right hand right off the bat and dropped me. I said he closed his eyes and just threw his best overhand right as hard as he could and I was too tired, too lazy, too slow, too old to do anything about it. So he dropped me and I got up, of course, and fought on but never got my rhythm going until the fight was stopped and I told my best friend Steve, who was my only trainer that night, "I'm done, brother. I'm done. I'm tired. I don't, won't train anymore and Robin Rae has been telling me too for years now, but I'm done."

I'm not going to say anything bad about the guy, Mark De Mori, that beat me. He simply beat a 42- almost 43-year-old that did not train and drank on the plane on the way over. I just felt I was not going to be beat again, but I deserved to lose and congratulations, Champ. You Won.

I think losing this fight and still remembering how close I came until losing that fight in Germany against the Russian Alexeev was what drove me crazy for few years. That and telling Marshall I believe the guys in St. Louis will get us the fight we want. I now understand all I had to do was wait on the call prior to the Alexander fight and even the Alexeev fight. All I had to do was wait for the call for the WORLD CHAMPIONSHIP FIGHT. WE GOT ONE FOR $80,000 BUT IT WAS NOT ENOUGH, SO I WAITED AND TOOK THE FIGHT WITH ALEXANDER WITHOUT TELLING MARSHALL, AND THEN I TOOK ALEXEEV WHEN I DID NOT HAVE TO. I WAS WBC, WBA, IBF INTERNATIONAL CHAMPION STILL, BUT WHEN BILLS KEPT COMING, KIDS GROWING UP, BUILT TOO BIG HOME, HEALTH CLUB—TEAM CALLOWAY— CLOSING... IT WAS TOO MUCH. OH WELL, I JUST HAD FIGHT

#92 IN AUSTRALIA AGAIN. CRAZY TIME OF LIFE AND 42 years old. GLAD MY WIFE ROBIN RAE REDMOND CALLOWAY IS STILL WITH ME AFTER BEING MARRIED TO THIS CRAZY MAN FOR 24 YEARS NEXT WEEK.

ANYBODY TELL YOU THEY LOVE YOU TODAY, ROBIN RAE CALLOWAY? I DO!!!!

END OF MY 92 PROFESSIONAL FIGHT CAREER

ROB CALLOWAY, ALL AMERICAN PRIZEFIGHTER
76 Wins, 14 Losses, 2 Draws, 60 Wins by Knockout
Fought in over 20 different states
Fought 10 X outside of USA in 8 different countries: Denmark, Germany x 2, England, Australia x 2, Poland, Russia, China, Bahamas

ROUND 12

All American Prizefighter, Rob and Robin Rae Calloway married 24 years next month. JULY 6ᵗʰ, 1991.

I Promised Robin that I would retire for good and I did St. Patrick's Day 2012. Robin was tired of me fighting and tired of me being gone, tired of ring card girls, tired of stewardess on planes, tired of everything about the sport of Professional Boxing.

I REALIZED I WOULD MISS HER MORE THAN I WOULD MISS FIGHTING OR THE OTHER THINGS SHE MENTIONED AROUND THE WORLD. I LOVE MY WIFE ROBIN. THANK YOU FOR LOVING ME AND ALLOWING ME TO LIVE MY DREAM OF FIGHTING AROUND THE WORLD. THANK YOU FOR PUTTING UP WITH ALL THE BULLSHIT YOU PUT UP WITH FOR 20 YEARS. I HAVE ALWAYS AND WILL ALWAYS LOVE ONLY YOU, ROBIN RAE CALLOWAY.

I actually began training after getting several other offers, but I never took it serious enough until I was in the US Virgin Islands and got a call to come to South America for my seventh return from retirement. I got myself in shape while I was in the US Virgin Islands. I TOLD ROBIN, "I feel good and will go down and stay down if caught with anything crazy." She cried and said, "No, you won't. You keep fighting until you're hurt or dead if they don't stop it." Then she said, "Robbie, please. You don't train, no sparring, and what the hell is $40,000 going to do? You just made $50 an hour in the Virgin Islands and $40 as a traveling PTA, so just stick to that and I don't have to worry about the fighting anymore and everything that goes with the fighting that I CANNOT TAKE ANYMORE." I KNEW WHAT SHE WAS TALKING ABOUT AND I DID NOT EVER FIGHT AGAIN.

I LOVE MY WIFE—SHE STILL LOVES ME—AND I STILL LOVE HER: 2 ROB'S

I STRUGGLED FOR MONTHS WITH CONTINUING EDUCATION TO BE ABLE TO RECEIVE MY MISSOURI PHYSICAL

THERAPIST ASSISTANT LICENSE AGAIN. But, I DID get my license soon thereafter.

I was hired part-time by our local hospital Heartland Health in the Home Health department. M, W, F, but I was more lost than I realized as I needed time to learn how much Physical Therapy had progressed in the last 15 years. I had most the problem with my notes and trying to learn how to use the computer with their program, but I tried my best and was able to begin the next part of my life.

I struggled with not only working again in a real job, but also understanding I'm not the center of attention anymore, that I didn't deserve any more attention than anyone else received. Some or many people do not even like boxing or care about me OR LIKE ME. I now realized how spoiled I was, although I must admit it was a very hard transition.

I would like to thank the ones who were the most understanding and I consider friends like Scott Koelliker, Teresa Mihilski for giving me my first job, and the Physical Therapist I worked with after fighting for 20 years. Many more, but Life goes on…

Things were not so good for awhile………

'WE GET GOOD AT MAKING EXCUSES, IT'S DIFFICULT TO EXCEL AT ANYTHING ELSE. SO I WON'T…

Soon I was offered full -time job as a Travelling Physical Therapist Assistant for Med-Travelers and I accepted and told Robin Rae I guess I'll be working away from home again. She said, "You never complained about working away from home for 20 years when you were away Fighting." I realized she was right, and I also realized I needed to quit crying and feeling sorry for myself. "Be a Man, boy," my dad said to me when I was 9 years old. I guess I was still a boy at that time, but I've started acting or at least trying to act like a man ever since. So thanks, Dad.

I retired from boxing on St. Patrick's Day 2012. I started working as a travelling physical therapist October 25th, 2012, but the problem was there was too much time in between jobs so after several assignments, I decided to take my first full time job since 1999. I'm very happy now working my First Full Time Job in Physical Therapy here on the Gulf Coast of Texas.

I understand how much I had been spoiled, I guess, as I'm in a hotel alone. No one to get my drinks, dinner, take me to gym, train me, wake me up early to shower and get ready for work. But I sucked it up as I made myself more upset knowing I was being a baby.

I remember working in boxing camps for months then fighting for $10,000 to $120,000 and I would always try get it in cash if possible and if not, I would get at least $20,000 in cash so I could blow it like a Dumbass, buying drinks or souvenirs for family when none of them ever asked for anything. Well, Butter did, but I already had her some stuff in my bags. But now working 40 hours all week as traveler, I have been working now over three years and have never seen a dime as all the money is automatically transferred into bank account and we have debit cards to use for cash.

I remember when Robin and I were dating in the 80's, I took a job in the summer at a hog processing plant, Monfort Pork. I just remember getting a check each Friday and going to local bar in the south side of St. Joseph, Missouri and cashing it before going to see Robin Rae at the Snappy Apple, the fruit stand her dad had built for her and her sister Toni to run. It really was a moneymaker as with the two pretty girls selling fruit, I think all the men in St. Joseph were living healthier.

I was offered my first full-time job in Physical Therapy from Med Travelers, a company based in Dallas, Texas. I soon realized how big the state of Texas was—wow. Anyway my first assignment was in Mountain Home, Arkansas, which was only around a five-hour drive from our home in St. Joseph, Missouri, so I loved the location, as I was able to go home for the weekends. I had trouble all week getting accustomed to the computer systems but enjoyed the opportunity to return to Physical Therapy and realized I enjoyed the patient care and I enjoyed having the opportunity to help people. I was so glad I got my degree in PT. Although the city I loved and fought out of for 20 years did not feel I was worth spending some time helping me get accustomed to working after fighting over 20 years and making millions of dollars for the city of St. Joseph, Missouri, I had to quit crying and fight for my family, using my mind from now on. I did and I followed up Mountain Home with Dexter, Missouri, although Dexter was a further drive home than Mountain Home was for me. I had to send my resume to wherever I was hoping to get the next travel job, so of course it had on my resume my entire boxing career and the many achievements. So when I arrived, the Director of Rehabilitation already knew about my career and I guess shared with employees prior to me arriving. I loved it of course, as I have to admit one of the things I got used to was all the attention every single day and my life was all about me. My beautiful wife does not want to be the center of attention at all and could not understand me in so many ways.

Years ago when I was interviewing with media from my locker room prior to my biggest fight in my career at the at time, the KQ2 sports reporter said, "Rob what is your prediction of the fight?" My father-in-law 'Big Daddy' was standing right beside me when I said, "I'm going to KNOCK HIM OUT." Big Daddy said, "SONOFA-BITCH. YOU CAN'T SAY THAT. WHY IN THE HELL WOULD YOU PUT SO MUCH PRESSURE ON YOURSELF? AND ME?" Big Daddy worked my corner by himself that night and did a GREAT job just like I knew he would and I WON BY A 2nd ROUND KO. GREAT NIGHT AND WE NEVER SLOWED DOWN. AND BIG DADDY ALWAYS LET ME RUN MY MOUTH.

HE WOULD ABSOLUTELY LOVE OUR KIDS NOWADAYS. CHASE THE FIGHTER LIKE ME, ONLY QUIET AND NICE LIKE HIS MOMMA AND BUTTER ATHLETIC LIKE US BOTH AND NOT AFRAID TO TELL YOU SHE'LL KNOCK YOU OUT, I GUESS TOO.

My next travel assignment in Physical Therapy was in the US VIRGIN ISLANDS. I KNOW, TOUGH JOB, but the Virgin Islands Physical Therapy and Sports Rehabilitation Clinic needed a LPTA and my recruiter, Raffinae Sanders from Dallas, let them know the champ was available as she was a fan. Well, her husband was and told her who I was after she told him her new client was Rob Calloway from

St. Joseph, Missouri who was professional boxer 20 years.

The greatest thing about my experience in the USVI was the day I arrived at the clinic the PT Maritza said, "Rob, this first week is *Carnival*, which is the island's anniversary, so we won't work until next week. I went all over the island from one party to the other with live bands on every corner and I will admit to drinking too much rum. Lots of rum...

I had a great experience working on the island, but I will say the most difficult part was learning to drive on the left side of the road across the small curvy mountainous roads everyday from my condo on the beach to work in the city, about a 20-minute drive over the island's mountain. I actually began to think, *OMG I really feel this is a better way to drive and I believe we have been driving on the wrong side of the road all these years.* I got to meet and speak with some famous professional boxers from the islands like Julian Jackson, who was a Don King fighter and very good middleweight. I worked in the US Virgin Islands Sports Rehab Clinic, which was right next to the US Virgin Islands Hospital where I ate lunch daily.

I look forward to bringing my wife Robin with me to the Virgin Islands some day. Now that our kids are both in college, she will have no excuse not to go with me.

My next assignment was in Carthage, Texas not too far from where I'm at now at my first full-time position in years. I was still having trouble understanding all the different computer softwares and this was a new company who used Therapute, however I would be with this company for the next few assignments in Texas and I began to understand and like the software.

My next travel Physical Therapy Assignment was in Amarillo, Texas, up from San Antone. Everything that I had was just what I had on. OKAY Lil George Strait—The Champ.

I still have a good friend that I keep in touch with, Adam, from Amarillo. I hope you're doing well and ready for me to beat you in a game of 21 Basketball again too. One of these days we will play again!!! Got To. I'd love for your Pretty wife to meet my Pretty wife; I have a feeling they would get along well.

One day maybe, Brother. Keep punchin', Champ.

I got my next assignment even closer to where I am now in my permanent position in Hemphill, Texas near Louisiana. I actually stayed in Louisiana and drove to work in Texas each day. I continued to realize I enjoyed working with the elderly and everyplace I went, I know the patients enjoyed having me there to help them in their rehabilitation. I loved talking with all the old men and many would become my friends who enjoyed sitting around even after hours with me telling them stories of the many fights I had all over the world.

One assignment led to the next and I spent a few months in southern Texas getting to know a permanent PTA who lived in Louisiana. I stayed at his place before finding a cabin to rent on the lake as there are some really huge lakes in south Texas/Louisiana that lead right down to the gulf of Mexico. I have to say I love my wife Robin Rae Redmond Calloway more than anyone in the world and I never want to lose her. We'll be married 24 years next month, but I had the hardest time being the husband I should be, working with all the travelers from across the country as there are just not any Physical Therapy or Occupational Therapy or Speech Therapist Universities in the area that offer an opportunity to get a degree in these areas, therefore requiring the hospitals to get therapists from travel companies like the one that sent me there, Med Travelers, or one of the so many more I've learned about over the last three years.

Well, I was in Hemphill, Texas next to some huge lakes in Louisiana as I worked right on the Texas/Louisiana border in the hospital and stayed with a full time therapist, who had moved there permanently from Alabama.

I was able to meet a few good people on my travel assignments, like Josh from Many, Louisiana or My Man Adam in Amarillo, but I wanted to return home to be with my wife, Robin Rae Calloway, who I still love more than anything in the world. I left the travel job without giving notice—I was crazier than I had ever been, traveling for two years, retired from fighting for good, losing last two fights, 43 years old. Then I took the job my recruiter, Raffinae Sanders, got me in St. Croix, Wisconsin, just over the state line from Minneapolis, Minnesota. I really liked the job and the people, but I felt like I was a southern boy and was ready to take a full time position I was offered after this travel assignment ended.

I'm on the Gulf Coast in Orange, Texas working full time now. I've had the chance to work with some great people here. Just needed my wife Robin Rae to be with me. AS THIS BOOK GOES TO PRESS, I'VE JUST BEEN OFFERED A JOB IN MISSOURI, CLOSE TO HOME. I'M SO EXCITED AND GRATEFUL TO BE ABLE TO COME FULL CIRCLE BACK TO MY ADOPTED HOMETOWN OF ST. JOSEPH, MISSOURI!

I got to live a dream. I remember Big Daddy saying, "Rob, it seems like 30 minutes ago I was riding my bike down King Hill Avenue, and now here I am with you, taking you to fight all over the Midwest and I'm 60. You think I'm crazy now but just wait and see how fast time goes by." He said so many things that I believed and learned from and repeated, but it seems a hell of a lot longer than 30 minutes ago since I had rode a bike down King Hill Avenue and I'm only 45 years old, Big Daddy. I loved Jerry 'Big Daddy' Redmond. RIP, CHAMP AND THANKS FOR EVERYTHING. AND I STILL LOVE YOUR BEAUTIFUL DAUGHTER ROBIN RAE REDMOND CALLOWAY!!! YOU WOULD BE SO PROUD OF YOUR GRANDKIDS, CHASE AND RILEY RAE. YOU WERE RIGHT AGAIN, CHASE HAS 120 FIGHTS RIGHT NOW AND HOPES TO MAKE THE 2016 OLYMPIC TEAM AND IF HE DOESN'T, HE WILL MAKE THE 2020 TEAM AND PROBABLY HAVE 200 AMATEUR FIGHTS. A LOT MORE THAN ME, JUST LIKE YOU SAID AND RILEY RAE LOVES TO SING AND DANCE AND ENJOYS THE SPOTLIGHT AND IS BEAUTIFUL LIKE ROBIN. OKAY, JUST LIKE YOU SAID, ROBIN AND I MARRIED 24 YEARS THIS JULY SIXTH. SHE IS STILL THE PERFECT WIFE AND MOTHER. OKAY, JUST LIKE YOU SAID.

I always did my best. I want to give my wife Robin the best of me for the rest of my life.

St Joseph, Missouri to Orange, Texas, between Lake Charles, Louisiana and Beaumont, Texas and back to St. Joseph, Misouri.

I Thank GOD for giving me an opportunity to live such a blessed life with my beautiful healthy family and all the friends I've been able to meet all over the world. I used to think the world is SO BIG. Now I realize how SMALL the WORLD is…

Thank you for reading my Book!

Anybody told you they love you today, Robin, Chase, and 'Butter'????
I DO!!!

ALL AMERICAN PRIZEFIGHTER
ROB CALLOWAY

2022 BOXING HALL OF FAME CANDIDATE

I love my wife so much for all the sacrifices she has made for over 25 years being my girlfriend and wife, as she not only allowed me to put boxing first but she helped me be as successful as I could be by always supporting my career and all the meals, vitamins, water, juice, energy drinks she would make sure I had. I was so blessed to have met Robin Rae Redmond Calloway at such an early age and fall in love and marry her on July 6th, 1991.

About the Author:

Rob Calloway is an American boxer. He had forty amateur bouts, being the Kansas City Golden Gloves champion two times and a USA Regional Champion in St Louis, which led eventually to the semifinals for the 1992 US western Olympic trials.

He has held the World Boxing Council Continental Americas Title, the WBA and IBF International titles. His World Heavyweight Championship win over Bob Mirovic in Australia, on the Gold Coast, for the World Boxing Foundation heavyweight championship was designated the 2005 Fight of the Year by Fox Sports (Australia). Calloway has fought on HBO Europe, PPV, Showtime, Fox Sports and on ESPN 6 times, winning Five.

Rob Calloway took the name of the All American Prize Fighter after his adopted hometown of St Joseph, Missouri won an All American City Award in 1996. Rob has received a Key to the city and a Day in Honor from his adopted hometown.

Calloway has fought in over 20 different states and 10 Times Outside of the USA in 8 different countries: 2X in Germany and 2X in Australia, Denmark, England, Poland, Bahamas, China, and Russia.

Calloway has faced some of the world's most famous boxers, including former heavyweight champions Hasim Rahman, Shannon Briggs, and Russia's Ruslan Chagaev two times with the first being a Technical Draw on Showtime. Chagaev knocked out Calloway in two rounds in the rematch in Germany in his fight before winning the WBA World Heavyweight Championship.

Calloway and his wife Robin of 24 years have two children, Chase ("Kid Dynamite") Calloway 19yo, who has over 120 amateur Bouts thus far and plans to make the 2020 USA Olympic Boxing Team and Riley Rae Calloway 18yo. Riley is also an athlete who excels in Dancing and Track at the college level in Kansas.

Calloway Retired St Patrick's Day 2012' after 20 Years and his 92nd Professional Fight and 2nd in the Country of Australia.

He now administers Physical Therapy in Orange, Texas. Rob received his college education prior to turning professional in 1992.

A Message From the Author:

Thank you for taking the time to read my book. I would be honored if you would consider leaving a review for it on *Amazon*.

Acknowledgements

I wrote my story for myself to always have a biography of the last 20 years of fighting all over the world as a professional. I can live with myself because I did the very best I could do after the first bell rang until the last or the fight ended by knockout. I always did my best! I love my wife Robin and I always wanted to win for her as she sacrificed more than anyone and always supported me 100%. I fought hard as possible for my son Chase after he was born in 1995 knowing he was watching on TV or would soon on tape just as my little girl Riley Rae, born in 1997, would. I thank these three as although many other things along my career inspired me to train and want to win, it was these three I thought of once I climbed through the ropes, ready to give all I could! 100% All American Prizefighter 76-14-2...60 KO's.

Special thanks to:
Jerry 'Big Daddy' Redmond,
You accepted me when I was teenager telling you I was gonna graduate college, become a boxing Champion, and Love Your daughter forever. Robin always believed in me and so did you! I Loved you like a father. You taught me so much on all our boxing trips around the country. Thank You seems so little to say for your believing and trusting in me but Thank You for being, besides Robin, my biggest fan and your loving and believing in me allowed and made me be my best. Your son wore your Lil white hat in my corner when I won the World Championship in Australia so it would remind me of you and your belief in me to one day become a world boxing champion. I Will Always Love You and Your Beautiful Daughter Robin Rae! You gave her the name and told me you was proud of the father and husband I am. I wish you had told her you love her more, so I do all the time for us both. You said you were proud of the father I am, which makes me wanna do better. Riley Rae says "I know, Dad" when I tell her I love her everyday because I remember you said you wished you told Robin Rae more like I tell our kids! You told me you were proud I became a good heavyweight because you didn't think I'd be any bigger than Cruiserweight, which was 190lb at that time and I felt you in my corner seeing Jason wearing your Lil white cap the night I won the 2005 Fox Sports Fight of the Year in Australia! Thanks for everything! You believed and gave me the Chance to live my dream and become all I wanted!!! Great grandfather to your grandkids and great husband to your beautiful daughter with her big brown chocolate pie eyes you loved, and I do too. Thanks Big Daddy!

My brother-in-law, Jason Redmond,

Jason and I were very close for many years. I loved watching his HS Football games and coaching him from the corner of many amateur and professional boxing matches. He was always a smart young man and helped Robin and me own and operate Team Calloway Family Health and Fitness Club 11 Years. He did an awesome job working many of my professional fights, including me winning the Fox Sports 2005 Fight of the Year on Gold Coast of Australia. My Lil Brother Jason and I have been together since day one. He went with me and Big Daddy to KC when buying everything for the gym so I could train at home in St Joseph and Jason trained right along with me, even lacing on the sparring gloves several times. He would learn so much by being quiet and listening and I learned by talking a lot, asking questions, sometimes same one over and over until I understood, but we each had our method to gain as much information about the sport of boxing as we could. I told Big Daddy Jason can fight; I've held the mitts and trained him some. He said, "No, I don't want him fighting" then after I showed him mitt work, etc, next time we were in KC, he let him spar and watched 1,000 times because he was so proud of him and Ilene was too. Jason was always in my corner until I stepped to next level training in Philadelphia and he did not go on the last two fights of my career in China and back in Australia, but he was great in my victory in Australia in my World Championship fight.

My mother-in-law, Ilene,
Thank you for putting up with me, Big Daddy, and your baby Jason travelling all over to fight and also always having something in the "pot" to eat when we got back. Thanks also for helping us out at Team Calloway, working the desk or anything else we needed. You're the best and you have seen it all.

My Mother, Patricia Sue,
I Love you and thank you for passing on genes that help make me a world champion. Thank You for coming to watch me fight when you could, I appreciate and Robin and I as well as your grandchildren Chase and Riley Rae Love You. You have always been there for me and for US and I thank you and will always Love and Respect You for everything. You help make me become the Champion I made of myself. I Love You MOM. THANK YOU!!

My Father, Mike Calloway,
I Love you and thank you for passing on genes that help make me a world champion. Thank you for coming to watch me fight when you could, I appreciate you and so do Robin and your grandchildren, Chase and Riley Rae. Love You.

My sister-in-law, Toni Redmond,
Thank You for bringing your sister Robin Rae to Bonnie and Clyde's in 1988 and Here's to Another 30 Years!

Jon Koelliker,
Jon was my Best Man in wedding, my assistant trainer in amateurs as well as many professional fights and even cut man for several. I Loved Jon. He was a great friend for many years.

Steve Ward,
Steve Ward was a long-time friend who always loved boxing and wrestling and even promoted his share of both. Years later in my boxing career, we soon became best friends and he was there in my corner at my greatest times when I won the World Championship in Australia. He was there in some of my worst times during my defeats in Russia Poland China and my last fight ever #92 in Australia.

Big Ed Davis,
I loved Big Ed. He was a great friend! I'll never forget the first time Big Daddy brought him to the Holiday Inn when the team and I were upstairs in the suite getting ready to leave for the fight at the arena and Big Daddy said he wants Big Ed with us and he will be great and he was so right! Soon big Ed became one of the most important guys on the team. Always there for me if I needed the food and drink bag carried or for him to drive me somewhere or to be Head of Security, which was the nickname he earned for remainder of my career. I remember when we fought Rock in Baltimore and Robin had us all dressed alike in our red, white, and blue and his crew gave Big Ed a hard time at first but could tell he was a great guy and we all had his back just like I always knew Big Ed had my back or my wife or son or daughters!!! Great important member of Team Calloway! Head of Security

Dr. Jimmy Albright,
I loved Dr. Jimmy and so did my wife Robin who always sent him back soon as she saw him to pray with the team and me!!! I always felt great after he prayed and I guess shared with Robin and I think she always felt better knowing he was back there!!!

Dick and Mignon DeShon,
Robin and I both will always love Dick and Mignon DeShon! Robin and I would cruise through town and Riley Rae already fell asleep but Chase would sit up in his seat and say DICK and MICK's house... He was little, of course, but Dick and Mignon and I and Robin all loved it!!! One day at church, Mignon said she enjoyed watching me on TV, saying how much I loved my wife and wanted to win because with time away training, I felt I needed too. Dick said, "Hey, I wanna meet the champ" so they became our biggest fans from riding in a bus to watch me win my first title in the Heavyweight division shown on PPV back home to Dick flying with

rest of crew from St. Joseph who was on a charter plane to Boise, Idaho while Mignon and her friend Jan Pray drove from St. Joseph, MO to Boise to watch my 12-round world title fight with Kenny Keene. We called them Thelma and Louise and we all loved them for being there.

Dick Rochambeau,
Dick Rochambeau was a guy who was such a sweet man and friend to my father-in-law Big Daddy as both had businesses in downtown St. Joseph for years. Dick would even come watch me train years ago with Big Daddy in the early 90's and soon was one of my best fans and friend to me and my wife along with his lovely wife and daughter too. I loved him like a family member and to me and Robin, he always will be. Thanks for always buying tables to fights and thank you to Dick Rochambeau Dick DeShon, Doug Stokes, David Lee Reynolds, and Bob Norton for all helping us start our dream Team Calloway Family Health and Fitness Club.

David Lee Reynolds,
What a great friend he was. I loved David and one day at the YMCA after Big Daddy had me running around the track throwing punches, we caught his eye. Later we were in the hot tub together and soon we spoke about both being from Louisville, KY and loving boxing so we shared stories. He said you're a little old at 19 to be just starting boxing, but he became a bigger fan every fight and I cried when we lost him! Robin and I Love You, Champ! Thank You!

John Gillaspie
So many great memories!
Thank you for being a great boss as PT who first hired me and becoming best friend, showing how to be a man providing for and loving my wife, taking care of kids, paying taxes, saving money, buying mutual funds, watching the Kansas State Wildcats, listening to country music. You're Awesome! I Love You, John, and Thanks for supporting my Boxing Career as I did my best every time I got into the ring!

Dr Juan Dominguez,
My Friend! I remember when we first bought our house and Dr. Juan was 5 doors down. Soon we got together, becoming friends and soon our wives as well and our children began to know each other. Juan and Veronica soon joined Team and always enjoyed doing our Box Aerobic class I made up, soon bringing other friends. Juan became our Physician on Fight night and I was so proud he agreed to come along as part of our team to Baltimore when I fought Hasim 'Rock' Rahman leading to many great nights along my entire career. Thanks Champ! Thank you for all your help and friendship! We Love You!

Dr Don Gossit

Thank You for being My Friend and I'll never forget us calling you on our way home from England after my broken jaw and you fixing the next morning after coming to see me late at night when we got home. I remember you saying you go to same church as we did and you where always so kind giving me your time! I was proud you even sat in corner my first fight back from broken jaw. You weren't real happy as you had already fixed my jaw after me breaking wires from gritting teeth, then again from jumping too much which made you put staples as well as the wires, Then again a month later, I broke playing Basketball at Team Calloway so you wired, staples, and ran a wire up around nose bone to keep my big mouth shut for good and it worked! My Friend for life then kind enough to help in corner my first fight back against 7'2 Julius Long from Detroit and being there for me while I won unanimous 12 round decision. Thank You and of course Robin and I Love and Thank You!

Dr Ed Friedlander,

The KC Fight Doctor, My Friend, Dr. Ed Friedlander who I met as he became My Friend from seeing pic and loved my Flat Top haircut just like he had. He began following my career and soon we asked him to be the fight Doctor for one of our bouts. Then he began following our son Chase and enjoyed the competitiveness of amateur boxing but more importantly, the way fighters love and aspirations to become a champion in worlds toughest sport. He loved seeing my soft side towards my kids and my wife yet willing to Fight in ring and beat some of toughest men in world. He soon began working donating his time to the Kansas City golden gloves and I was so glad we became great friends to this day and he is friend and fan our son Chase and has always loved Robin and our daughter Riley Rae. Besides my father n law years ago Doc was the one who encouraged me to write My Story of my life and boxing career. Thank You Doc as it has been great for me while being away from my family these last 3 years on the road returning to work in physical therapy after fighting professionally 20 years! My Friend for life and I plan to write boxing instruction book after releasing All American Prizefighter again thanks to your encouragement! God Bless Champ and Thank You!

My Nieces and Nephews I hope that you guys are all great. I haven't got to know my family on My Side as I moved to MO at a young age and got my education, played college basketball one year and lived a dream come true becoming the All American Prizefighter but I know my mother sister and brothers have shared My Story all through your lives! I'm glad you got to see anything is possible through hard work and believing you can do anything. I Love you and hope I've left good memories for each of you as well as Robin's Nieces and Nephews who I have Loved their whole life! I Love my wife's nieces and nephews and again I'm Proud of each one! I love seeing your success and the love each of you show for your children! Makes Uncle

Rob Proud and I Love it when Lil Dave still calls me Uncle Robbie!!! Even though he is in his mid 30's!!! Love it!!
 We even have great nieces and nephews now and I love so much and look forward to seeing more often very soon!!! Believe!! Work hard and get your education!!! My Champs!

My sister! I Love You Kimmy! You're a great mother, wife, daughter and sister and I appreciate you becoming such a great person! My wife Loves You and I know You Love Robin and Thank You for being a great sister to her Too.

John and Pat, Thank you for being Great Fathers and Husbands, great sons to mom and yes great brothers to Robin Rae and me. We Love You.

I Love My Family and remember my cousins and so happy for all of your success. You all make me Proud!

So many great friends and fans! Thank You! I wanna say so much more but really just Thank You! Thanks for being apart of my fights my life and nothing feels better than being at Walmart and having kids under age 10, who I'm sure never saw me fight but only heard stories from their parents, and they come shake my hand get my autograph and I give them hug and say Thanks because it means More To Me!!! Love everyone! Worth 92 professional fights all over world!!!

I want to say a Special Thank You to my Editor and Publisher Julie Casey, who Robin and I have known and loved for 20 years. She was our kids' preschool teacher and now she and her husband will publish my book with their company Amazing Things Press. Life has came in a full circle it seems, as now we are publishing a book together and both our children, who called Julie 'JuJu,' are now in College. Time flies and Thank God for Family and Friends. Blessed

Check out these books from
Amazing Things Press

Keeper of the Mountain by Nshan Erganian

Rare Blood Sect by Robert L. Justus

Survival In the Kitchen by Sharon Boyle

Stop Beating the Dead Horse by Julie L. Casey

In Daddy's Hands by Julie L. Casey

MariKay's Rainbow by Marilyn Weimer

Convolutions by Vashti Daise

Seeking the Green Flash by Lanny Daise

Thought Control by Robert L. Justus

Tales From Beneath the Crypt by Megan Marie

Fun Activities to Help Little Ones Talk by Kathy Blair

Bighorn by James Ozenberger

Post Exodus by Robert Christiansen

Rawnie's Mirage by Marilyn Weimer

Fall of Grace by Rachel Riley and Sharon Spiegel

Taming the Whirlwind by Lindsey Heidle